And Other Surprises!

by Cathy Lee Phillips

Patchwork Press, Ltd.
Canton, Georgia
www.patchworkpress.com
770-720-7988

SILVER IN THE SLOP

And Other Surprises!

First Printing 1999
Second Printing 2001
Third Printing 2004

Library of Congress Catalog Card Number: 99-70343

Published by:
Patchwork Press, Ltd.
P. O. Box 4684
Canton, Georgia 30115

ISBN 0-9715925-0-0

Printed in the USA by
Morris Publishing
3212 East Highway 30 – Kearney, NE 68847 – 1-800-650-7888

With Love to Jerry,

- *For the friendship that was the foundation of our love. . .*
- *For teaching me, once and for all time, what a real family is all about . . .*
- *For laughing with me when life was joyous . . .*
- *For holding me when life was cruel . . .*
- *For showing me the real meaning of courage . . .*
- *For living your faith at all times . . .*
- *For pink roses and blue butterflies . . .*
- *For loving me with an unconditional love . . .*
- *For the way you are still with me today. . .*

God blessed me with a trough-full of silver
When He brought you into my life!

TABLE OF CONTENTS

TABLE OF CONTENTS

Foreword

It may seem a bit of a stretch to argue that this book is in the tradition of Martin Buber, Paul Tillich, and Brother Lawrence, but in truth it is. Buber spoke of "hallowing the everyday," encouraging us to encounter the holy in daily living, to meet "The Eternal Thou" in the persons we find in our offices, homes, schools or places of relaxation. Similarly, Tillich contended that the events of our lives have a theonomous depth because God is the very ground of all that is. Brother Lawrence lived out these truths, finding and serving God as much in sweeping a kitchen floor as in times of prayer and worship.

Now comes a delightful collection of stories by Cathy Lee Phillips built upon this tradition – but with a difference. Her stories are easily read, sometimes mixing humor with wisdom, sometimes joining sorrow with inspiration. These vignettes have a "me too" character. As we read about her being caught with an empty candy wrapper during a time of dieting, those of us who know the temptations that accompany attempts at weight control find ourselves not only laughing at Cathy's rationalization but saying "me too" and laughing at our own foibles. In a story about a retreat following her husband's death, Cathy draws us into her feeling of emptiness and draws out of us our own encounters with loss and questioning of faith.

Cathy Lee Phillips' life is like her writing – diverse and joyous. I first met her when she was a student at Scarritt

Graduate School, where she was "into" everything, from pranks that made us all a bit nervous to serving as president of the student body. She had previously won a typing contest in Georgia, and we dubbed her "the fastest fingers in the south." She is also fast with her head and heart. She has an unusually keen ability to share her zest for life so that our lives are enhanced. She invites us to laugh and cry with her so that we open ourselves to greater joy. She helps us look at the events of our lives so that we encounter deeper meaning.

Using her life experiences, Cathy leads us to find joy and meaning in the midst of our daily living. One of her pieces, "Silver in the Slop," captures the thrust of her message. When she was a young girl, her family would gather the garbage from a fine restaurant to supplement feed for their hogs. The pigs ate the food scraps, but they left certain indigestible objects in the bottom of their trough -- fine polished silverware. Cathy Lee Phillips' life is like that. She is determined to find valuables among the seemingly invaluable, blessings among trials, joy in the midst of pain, wisdom in the commonplace, and God in the everyday.

Read these stories and meet Cathy. Be entertained with fun and instructed with serious reflection. Read these stories and meet yourself. Recall your own temptations, joys, sorrows, and inspirations. Read these stories and meet your Lord. Find God in the fun, struggles, and even refuse of life.

James I. Warren, Jr.
The Intentional Growth Center
Lake Junaluska, North Carolina

Acknowledgements

"Write what you know!"

That is what the experts tell you – and that is what this book is all about.

You will quickly see that what I know includes growing up on a farm and cherishing the unique education it affords. I know about maneuvering the rocky roads of childhood and adulthood. I know about working your way through school to do what you feel called to do. I know about marrying the man you love, then loosing him too soon. I know about grief and the struggle to upright your world when it has suddenly been turned upside-down. I know about the times when God seems so near you can touch Him. I know about the lonely times when He seems far away and unreachable. I know about holding tightly to your dreams and working to make them a reality. I know the importance of family, but I am also painfully aware that no family is perfect. I know that family is not so much a product of biology as it is mutual respect, forgiveness, and unconditional love. I know the importance of hugs and laughter and the need for an ample supply of both.

I know that extraordinary lessons can be learned in the routine events of our lives – the good, the bad, and the ordinary. That is what this book is all about -- learning our lessons well and finding the silver in the slop. You have done this yourself, no doubt, and have countless stories you could share with me. These just happen to be my stories.

Writing has always been a part of my life. In fact, I see a story in just about everything. Some of these pieces were written years ago; others are quite new. I share these stories when I lead retreats, teach Sunday School, or speak in various capacities. The positive responses I have received, in fact, have given me the confidence I needed to go forth with this project.

For their continued encouragement, my sincere love and appreciation goes to my *family of choice* – Deborah, Drew, Jennifer, Dick, Allen, Kerry, Janice (self-appointed editor and Victory's godmother), Mike, Lynn, Nicholas, Toni, Bill, Glenda, Gary, Allison, Jim, Anna, James, William, Don, Betty, Sybil, Raleigh, The Stroud Clan who has known me forever, and certain members of the "Million Dollar Choir" (you know who you are!). And to the Baltes, Johnson, and Sosebee people – thanks for coming onboard!

To Jimmy and Marty, thank you for the calls and jokes that came at just the right moments. To the congregation of Orange United Methodist Church, thank you for sustaining Jerry and me during the most trying moments of our lives. To my new friends in South Carolina, thank you for reading these pages, correcting them, and laughing and crying at all the right places. To Neil, thank you for your insight and encouragement. I am a better person because of you.

To Dr. James I. Warren, my professor and friend, you have honored me deeply by writing the foreword for this book. Your wisdom, your knowledge, and your humor have blessed me for many years.

Finally, I would like to thank the many who have purchased this book and, thereby, made yet another printing necessary and possible. Thank you for letting me know you have enjoyed these stories. Your calls, letters, e-mails, and cards, have ministered to me at all the right moments. The many invitations to lead your retreats and speak at your various functions have only confirmed that this book was meant to be. I am blessed by knowing that you laugh and cry right along with me. Thank you for inviting my book and me into your lives!

"Write what you know," the experts say.

This is what I know. Welcome to my world – I pray you are able to both laugh at my goofs and learn from my lessons. This is the stuff of life!

Now, to all the people mentioned above – the book is finished. LET'S PARTY!

Cathy Lee Phillips
Canton, Georgia
February 2001

SILVER IN THE SLOP

Negotiations had been lengthy and intense, but after four slices of pecan pie and six glasses of iced tea, a handshake sealed the agreement. Beginning the following Sunday, our pigs would feast thrice weekly on slop from the Newnan House Restaurant.

One of the oldest restaurants in the county, the Newnan House had an unbeatable reputation. The restaurant served thick steaks, fried green tomatoes, and all the blueberry muffins you could eat. Consequently, most everyone found money to eat at the Newnan House Restaurant at least once a month.

Over the years, Daddy and Mr. Marrott, the owner, had become close friends. As their friendship grew, so did our invitations to free dinners at the Newnan House Restaurant. It was on one of these occasions that the post-dinner conversation, oddly enough, turned to slop.

Mr. Marrott had a problem. As his restaurant had grown, so had the quantity of table scraps deposited in large buckets outside his kitchen each week. The area was smelly, dirty, and a home to flies and other buzzing creatures. Even the presence of an expensive electric "bug zapper" did little to eliminate the problem.

What Mr. Marrott saw as a nuisance, though, Daddy saw as great fortune for the pigs that populated our Posey Road farm. Thus, the discussions began and by evening's end, Daddy and the pigs were proud recipients of prime Newnan House Restaurant slop. While the pigs would most likely have settled for anything, Daddy was a stern negotiator and held out for the very best – the Sunday afternoon slop (Sunday Buffet), the Tuesday slop (All-You-Can-Eat Fried Chicken), and the Friday slop (Catfish Night).

Three times each week on the aforementioned days, Daddy drove the old green GMC pickup truck on his "slop runs." Tied securely to the back of the truck were three 55-gallon drums – dirty, odorous, empty, and just waiting to be filled with first-rate Newnan House Restaurant slop.

I usually accompanied Daddy on the Sunday adventure around 4:00 in the afternoon. Wearing old shorts and a T-shirt, my bare feet swinging from the musty seat of the old truck, I sat next to the open window, the wind blowing the ragged edges of my pixie haircut.

The truck made a loud roaring noise because of several quarter-sized holes in the muffler. The gears shrieked painfully every time Daddy shifted from second to third. The giant green steering wheel had so much play in it that even when we were driving in a straight line, Daddy perpetually wrestled the wheel from side to side in a wide motion that barely kept the truck on the road.

But, there I sat, happy and proud to be a vital part of the Sunday afternoon slop run.

Just as we topped Wahoo Hill on Highway 29, we turned left into the Newnan House Restaurant parking lot and drove slowly toward the kitchen door. Scrambling into my usual position, I perched on my knees facing the back of the truck. I draped my arms over the back of the seat and pressed my nose against the rear window. Two cooks wearing dirty aprons and black hair nets directed Daddy alongside a concrete porch outside the kitchen. A unique and indescribable aroma burned my eyes and nose. Flies soared persistently around the kitchen until they naively wandered into the purple rays of the electric bug zapper. With a loud pop they fell like great war planes crashing into the sea.

The slop exchange took only minutes as Daddy and several busboys dumped leftovers from the town's leading citizens into the 55-gallon drums tied to the back of the GMC. I took my seat as we slowly turned back onto Highway 29 and crept carefully down Wahoo Hill. Proud of his cargo, Daddy intended for every drop to arrive safely at its destination.

Once on Posey Road, Daddy steered the truck down the dirt trail leading to the concrete pigpen. He backed the truck toward the trough, stopping when the tailgate gently nudged the pen. Jumping from the front seat, I climbed atop the pigpen and watched Daddy empty buckets and buckets of old steaks, congealed salads, fried okra, and such into the trough. Standing back, we smiled as we watched those pigs, well, be pigs. They ate every bite with great joy and unrestrained pleasure. My favorite part of the afternoon, though, was still to come!

While the pigs slurped and chewed and guzzled and the slop disappeared, strange and beautiful objects slowly began to emerge and sparkle in the summer sunshine. When the pigs finished their Sunday feast, lying in the bottom of the trough were assorted pieces of genuine Newnan House Restaurant silverware. Knives, teaspoons, salad forks, serving spoons – several pieces were accidentally tossed into the slop each week by busboys working feverishly to keep pace with the Sunday crowd. Mr. Marrott was too busy to be concerned with the loss of a few stray pieces of silverware.

"Better to loose a knife or fork than a customer. Keep the pieces," he said.

Rescued from the slop and scrubbed clean (several times!) our silverware collection grew steadily by three or four pieces each week. By the end of the first summer, an entire setting for eight, plus serving pieces, lay securely inside our kitchen, second drawer from the top, next to the sink. We used the silverware at first only for special occasions. As the collection grew, however, we broke with convention and used the good stuff every day.

For years our family, friends, neighbors, even Mr. Marrott himself, ate meals with genuine Newnan Restaurant silverware rescued from the pig slop.

Now, over thirty years later, two Newnan House Restaurant teaspoons rest securely in my own kitchen, second drawer from the top, underneath the oven.

How I treasure these silver pieces ransomed from the slop so many years ago! Two little spoons remind that, even in the worst times and the most unexpected places, there are lessons to be learned and blessings to be discovered. God's presence abides even when the world seems merely a jumble of chaos and confusion.

Silver in the slop! It can always be found if we have the patience to wait, to watch, and to recognize God at work in each moment of our lives. Remembering this, I rest in the assurance that God's blessings, sparkling and eternal, dwell in the loneliest night, the coldest winter, and the deepest distress.

And we know that in all things
God works for the good of those who love him,
who have been called according to his purpose.

Romans 8:28
(NIV)

JANUARY ROSES

Author's Note:

Guideposts Magazine was like a member of the family during my childhood. For many years, my grandmother subscribed to this magazine and faithfully read each issue from cover to cover. Every few months she would mail old copies to my mother. Eventually the stories made their way into my hands. I'm quite sure my Grandmother never envisioned my writing for this celebrated publication. This story, therefore, is further proof that God does indeed work in mysterious ways! "January Roses" first appeared in the January/February 1997 Edition of Angels On Earth Magazine, a Guideposts Publication. I am grateful to the Guideposts organization for publishing this true story in 1997. It was an honor to work with the editors and staff. I am equally grateful to Guideposts for graciously allowing me to include "January Roses" in this book.

JANUARY ROSES

When I lost my husband early in 1992, I lost my companion, my lover, my best friend. Jerry died of complications from a heart transplant, and after only six years of marriage, I became a widow at the age of 35. We should have been laughing and looking forward to a long, happy life together. Instead the years ahead loomed like an endless, deserted highway.

As the initial numbness faded, sadness overwhelmed me and I sank into a depression that deepened with each passing month. Time was supposed to heal all wounds, but for me it was an enemy that carried Jerry farther away.

I had a strong faith. Jerry had been a minister, and I was a director of Christian education. Nevertheless, grief and loneliness overshadowed my faith, and the solace I had once found in God was gone.

Occasionally I was able to lose myself in my work or enjoy an evening out with friends, but as soon as I walked through the front door, the silent house reminded me of life without Jerry. I'd look at the piano and think of how he loved to hear me play and sing. The couch in the living room made me remember our evenings snuggled in front of the TV. Some nights I lay awake for hours, missing the warmth of Jerry's body beside me.

Special occasions – Valentine's Day, Jerry's birthday, our anniversary – were the most difficult. Even Thanksgiving and Christmas, with family dinners to distract me, were devoid of joy.

As the first anniversary of Jerry's death grew nearer I didn't want to think about what I was going to do. Should I pretend it was just another day? Should I spend the day looking through our photo albums, reliving happier times?

Finally I decided the only place I might find peace was the beach. It had always been a place of rest and serenity for me. I wanted to hear and feel the power of God's sea, to inhale the sharp, briny air. Maybe that would make me feel alive again, close to God again.

I made reservations at a hotel on Amelia Island, Fla., where I had stayed once. It seemed an ideal place for solitary reflection and renewal.

On the morning of January twelfth I awoke early in my hotel room, my mind flooded with memories of that day one year before. The brown warm-up suit Jerry wore in the hospital – a Christmas gift from me. The afternoon we spent together, sitting side by side on the starchy sheets of his bed, looking through the classifieds for a new puppy to keep me company while he recovered. Later, the emergency call from the hospital. The short drive there, which seemed to take an eternity. The stark words, "We couldn't bring him back."

I knew a walk along the Amelia Island shore would clear my head, so I forced myself to get out of bed. I looked through the window. A wall of thick gray fog had rolled in. The mist obscured everything – the water, the sand, the seagulls, even the hotel courtyard. A walk was out of the question.

Sliding open the glass door, I stepped out onto the balcony and slumped into a deck chair. *All I wanted to do was walk on the beach.*

I sat there glaring resentfully into the dense fog. Then, in the rhythmic rush of the waves against the shore, I thought I heard a whisper. Or was it the surf?

You can't see the water, but you know it is near.

What? Then I heard the words a second time.

You can't see the water, but you know it is near.

The words receded, and in that moment of quiet, I understood. I couldn't see the ocean through the fog. But I could smell its saltiness in the air. I could hear the sound of the surf and the cry of the seagulls. Wasn't it the same with God?

A soft knock at the door interrupted my thoughts. I was puzzled; I didn't know anyone on the island. A hotel maid walked in, holding a glass vase with a beautiful bouquet of pale pink roses.

"I thought you might like these," she said, setting the vase on a side table and rearranging the flowers.

I was stunned, and it must have shown on my face because she apologized. "I'm sorry," she said. "I didn't mean to startle you."

"It's not that," I said, unable to stop my tears.

"I found the roses in another part of the hotel," she said. "I can't explain it, but something told me to bring them to this room."

I looked at the bouquet more closely. *That's odd,* I thought. *Not a dozen. Not a half dozen. . . .*

Then I told her about Jerry, about my loneliness. As I poured my heart out to this stranger, the fog of pain lifted. "Jerry used to give me pink roses on special occasions," I said. "We would have celebrated our seventh anniversary this year."

The maid hugged me tight. "I know you're still grieving, but life is more than grief," she promised as she slipped out of the door.

Standing in the middle of my room, I stared at the bouquet. Seven pink roses. I heard the whisper once more: *You can't see the water, but you know it is near.*

Thank you, God, for telling me Jerry is safe with you, and I must go on. Thank you for the seven pink roses – and for the angel who delivered them.

Blessed are those who mourn,
for they will be comforted.

Matthew 5:4
(NIV)

DESPERATELY SEEKING THUMBELINA

Author's Note:

Two days after Jerry's death, I awoke at 4:30 a.m., my mind crowded with memories, disbelief, grief, and a growing list of things to do. One item on that list was to finalize the bulletin for Jerry's Memorial Service. I wanted to write something special for that bulletin – something that would capture Jerry's spirit, his humor, his giving nature, and his love for me.

After several false starts, all of which sounded cold and very "funereal," I glanced across the room and spotted the Christmas present Jerry had given me just a few days before – a Thumbelina doll! As a child, this was the doll I always wanted but never received. When I mentioned this to my husband, he launched a personal crusade to find this doll for me. His search was a success and he gave Thumbelina to me on our last Christmas together, just a few days before his death. It was the last gift he gave me and one I will always treasure.

Many people have asked for copies of this tribute. The story of Jerry's search made them smile and, for others, it stirred memories of the Thumbelina dolls in their own childhood.

DESPERATELY SEEKING THUMBELINA

In one of those silly husband-wife conversations we once shared, I told Jerry that when I was seven years old, I wanted a Thumbelina doll. Thumbelina was THE DOLL of the early 1960's. She was made of simple cloth and plastic with a pink wind-up button on her back. As the button unwound, Thumbelina's arms, legs, and head moved in "real baby-like" motion.

Whatever the reason, I never received a Thumbelina doll when I was seven. I managed to go on and lead a normal life!

However, a Thumbelina doll now sits atop our bed. On Christmas Eve this year, Jerry took my hand and presented me with a brightly wrapped package topped with two white bows. As I tore away the paper, he related his two-year search for Thumbelina. Two years! He visited toy stores, Wal-Marts, and K-Marts. He consulted the yellow pages and called toy manufacturers. He even interviewed small children in several counties, asking where he might find the elusive Thumbelina. In mid-October, just before he entered St. Joseph's Hospital in Atlanta with rejection of his new heart, he located the doll in Duluth, Georgia. He bought her and sat her aside until wrapping the precious gift and placing it under our tree.

It may seem silly for a 35-year-old woman to receive a doll for Christmas. But, in this simple doll I see love – a love that persisted through his two-year search to fulfill my childhood wish. I see the sincerity of a man who always wanted for me – and for each of us – the desires of our hearts. In Thumbelina I see his humor, his laughter, his giving nature. It reminds me how very much I was loved in this life. This precious little doll will forever be a tangible reminder of everything that was good and caring and sharing in Jerry Phillips.

I thank God for my husband, Jerry. We met here at Grace United Methodist Church a mere twelve years ago, but I have memories to last my lifetime. I can remember his faith, his sincerity, his special personality, and his humor. I thank God for each day of our marriage. I thank God for the United Methodist Church that brought us together and for the incredible friends who comprise our very large extended family. I thank God for the skilled and compassionate Transplant Services Team at St. Joseph's Hospital who gave us an extra twenty months together.

With the gift of a new heart on May 9, 1990, Jerry experienced a resurrection of sorts. With his death on January 12, 1992, he experienced his second, and best, resurrection. My pain is deep but my heart is filled with gratitude for both of these resurrections and for the presence of each of you who comes today to celebrate his life on earth and his new life in Christ.

Where, O death, is your victory?
Where, O death, is your sting?

I Corinthians 15:55
(NIV)

CORNBREAD: THE STUFF OF FRIENDSHIPS

It was a way of life. From time to time some of my dearest animal friends made the dreaded transition from pasture to freezer.

As the child of a farm family, you quickly learn not to become too attached to what will eventually become your meatloaf or pot roast. Nevertheless, some animals are unforgettable!

There was Beetlebomm the bull, a close friend who ate apples from my hand. There was Tootey-Belle, the three-legged calf who could outrun any other animal in the pasture. And, who could forget Ed the pig, famous for his habit of jumping out of the pen and chasing cars. They were a unique collection of characters, certainly, and there was cause for mourning when their fateful day arrived. Nevertheless, those days were inevitable and the table was abundantly filled during the following weeks and months.

It was during one of those weeks that Vicky and Dan Anderson dropped by one Tuesday evening just before dinner. Their timing was perfect! Our home was decorated with the addictive odors of pot roast and homemade biscuits. As they were seated, it was obvious that Vicky and Dan were not leaving and they, in fact, responded quickly to mom's dinner invitation. The evening was relaxing and enjoyable – so much so that the next evening, just before dinner, Vicky and Dan returned. My mother, being a wonderful hostess, was calm as she quickly thawed T-bones under hot running water. The dinner was delicious, Vicky and Dan said as they were leaving soon after dessert.

We were really surprised at seeing the Andersons two nights in a row. Even more surprising, though, was watching their now-familiar car turn into the driveway the following evening.

Vicky and Dan loved the pork chops on Thursday, the fried chicken on Friday, and the ham on Saturday. It was quite obvious that a pattern had developed that left my mother planning and cooking dinner for eight people. She decided to fight back!

Sunday arrived and, with it, Vicky and Dan. They walked into the kitchen and found my mother preparing cornbread.

"That's one of my favorites!" Dan bellowed as he seated himself at the table.

"I'm so glad," my mother responded, placing the cornbread and a huge bowl of pinto beans in the middle of the dining room table. She seated herself silently and moved only to butter her cornbread.

"Oh no," I groaned to myself, having a great hatred for pinto beans and cornbread. "Surely there is more on the way."

But there wasn't. Dan's smile faded as he silently partook of his less-than-exciting cuisine. Conversation at the table was strained and the Anderson's left quickly after dinner.

As I helped Mom clear the table, I asked, "Do you think they will be back tomorrow night?"

"Oh, I hope so," she smiled slyly, "we still have quite a few pinto beans.

Vicky and Dan did not return the next night nor the one after that. In fact, it was a very long time before we saw them again.

But that's okay because I learned a great lesson from them.

Pot roast friends are fine.

But help me, O Lord, to be a cornbread friend!

A friend loves at all times. . .

Proverbs 17:7
(NIV)

A BLESSING IN DISGUISE

As the forecasters debated just how far below zero the temperature would drop, I burrowed deeper beneath my two quilts and pink electric blanket. Perfect! I was blissfully warm, cozy, and safe despite the rapidly falling temperatures and the cold blowing wind.

But when the electricity began to flicker, worry crept into the cozy bed with me. Where would I go if the power went out in my apartment? Would my quilts keep me warm if the pink electric blanket proved useless? I had rushed home without stopping at the grocery store. Was there enough food to last if the power stayed off for several days? My little car was outside in the freezing nighttime temperatures. Was it filled with an adequate amount of anti-freeze? Would the battery survive the cold night?

Suddenly, a deep memory stirred and for a fleeting moment, I missed the old wood heater.

The wood heater.

It was a constant embarrassment to me during my growing-up years. I was sure we were the only family in Georgia to have such a monstrosity in the home. Not only was it an eyesore, it was an awful aggravation. Countless were the hours I spent in the woods with my father cutting wood and bringing it home with the tractor and wagon.

That chore always came on the afternoon I had the most homework or on the Saturday I had big plans.

As a result, I perfected the art of finding excuses not to go to the woods – stomach pains, headaches, leg cramps, heart attacks and rare tropical diseases. Whatever the ailment, I managed to contract it at least twice during my childhood. That heater continually made my life difficult. Yet no amount of whining or complaining could exorcise that demon from our house. It remained right in the middle of our living room – a massive, smoking reminder that a cold trip to the woods was not far away.

It was not until many years later that I experienced even the slightest appreciation for that heater.

As I crawled into bed one cold Sunday night in 1973, the weather report played softly in the background. It didn't sound good, at least to Mama and Daddy. To me, though, an advancing ice storm was a ticket to a school holiday. My prayers were fervent that winter night and I shouted with delight when the next morning dawned. The world stood crisp, cold, completely frozen. When the radio announced, "NO SCHOOL," I wrapped myself in a patchwork quilt and settled down for some serious TV-watching.

Days of Our Lives had barely begun when the power flickered once, twice, then failed completely.

That was all. No television, no lights, no radio. Nothing worked for four days. Nothing, that is, except the ugly wood heater puffing away, fighting furiously to keep the ice and cold from over-taking our living room.

We boiled milk on the heater for hot chocolate. At dinnertime we learned that the wood heater provided an adventurous way of cooking everything from hotdogs to baked potatoes. For days, that heater was the most popular resident of Posey Road, heating and cooking for our family as well as various friends and relatives seeking warmth and a hot meal.

The ice storm of 1973 is a memory now, but the wood heater remains a permanent member of the house on Posey Road.

Now, as an older and much wiser adult, I can finally acknowledge my appreciation for that old wood heater. It warmed me. It fed me. It taught me to look for the value in all things, realizing that all persons, no matter how seemingly unattractive or unappreciated, have talents and blessings to give.

The Lord does not look at the things man looks at.
Man looks at the outward appearance,
but the Lord looks at the heart.

1 Samuel 16:7
(NIV)

THE GREAT POSEY ROAD BOAT-LAUNCHING

"I think I will build me a boat," Davy announced.

I chuckled to myself and thought, "What does he know about building a boat?"

He surprised me, though, that thirteen-year-old brother of mine, with his diligence if not his maritime knowledge. For the next several days his after-school hours were abuzz with the sounds of hammers and saws, grunts and groans, as a vessel slowly emerged from the chaos.

It was a strange sight – somewhat a cross between a floating barge and a life raft. First, Davy found two large logs that he placed parallel to one another approximately five feet apart. Across these he attached old boards found in various hiding places around the farm. Then he covered it all with a rather nauseating mossy green paint. Finally, he did to that contraption whatever little boys do to boats to make them float. Patting his hound, Lester, Davy stood back and admired his work.

Indeed, he had a boat, one that even floated. But he was not satisfied. His forehead wrinkled as he slowly studied the monstrosity from all sides. From the kitchen window I watched quietly as he stroked his chin thoughtfully. Even Lester sat quietly as the young shipbuilder pondered his work.

Finally, an idea burst into his consciousness. Davy jumped up, seized a hacksaw, and began cutting a two-foot square opening in the bottom of the vessel.

I had to speak up.

"Any simpleton knows that a boat can't float with a hole in the bottom," I offered, trying to keep the laughter out of my voice. Lester barked in agreement.

"Just wait and see," my brother said somewhat impatiently. "Just wait and see."

I was more than skeptical to say the least.

"By the way," he asked seriously, "what should we name her?

My Brother's Big Old Goofy Idea was the first name that came to my mind. But, not wanting to hurt his feelings, I managed to keep my mouth closed.

While I questioned his strategy, I admired his persistence and imagination. After cutting the hole in the bottom of his boat, Davy attached two pedals and a bicycle chain to the unsightly thing. Frowning slightly, he bit his lip in deep concentration.

"It will never float," I thought to myself.

"It will float," he said, as if reading my mind. "I just wish I could think of a name."

My pessimism continued even as my brother made plans for an appropriate boat launching ceremony. It was scheduled for warm Sunday afternoon at the pond near our house. The guest list included Lester the Hound, Davy's best friend, Jeffrey, as well as Mama, Daddy, and other Posey Road dignitaries.

Following an appropriate boat-launching luncheon, the hour arrived. The day was sunny and clear with a gentle wind blowing from the east. The ceremony began promptly at 3:30 p.m. as my brother stepped to the edge of the water and spoke a few appropriate boat-launching words. Jeffrey played an appropriate boat-launching ballad on his new tape player. Then, with great reverence, I walked toward the craft and gently christened the *USS WHATSERNAME* with a two-liter bottle of Coca-Cola.

Once the ceremony ended, my brother and his First Mate Lester, happily sporting a three-cornered paper hat taped to his ears, climbed aboard. As Jeffrey pushed the vessel away from the shore, the little boat tilted, swayed, and appeared to be anything but sea-worthy. First Mate Lester barked in alarm, lay flat on the deck, and covered his head and three-cornered hat with shivering paws. All the while my brother, The Captain, smiled confidently and pedaled furiously. As his legs pumped, water splashed in every direction, soaking both The Captain and First Mate.

Once the boat floated farther from shore, however, the motion became smoother and the pedaling slowed to a rhythmic pump.

"I did it!" he shouted.

"He did it!" we shouted, and those ashore engaged in a mass of hugging, the likes of which had not been seen on Posey Road for some time.

First Mate Lester lifted his paws, raised his head, and barked with joyful confidence.

The maiden voyage of the *USS WHATSERNAME* lasted precisely 17 minutes. It was the first of many for the young Captain and his four-legged First Mate. Whether for pleasure voyages or fishing expeditions, the *WHATSERNAME* was soon joined by the *USS SWAMP RAT* and *USS POSEY QUEEN*. Each boat proved as sea-worthy as the first.

With regret, I remember my first reaction the day my brother announced he would build his boat. I regret that I voiced skepticism instead of encouragement. I regret that I voiced cynicism instead of inspiration.

But God, with wisdom and humor, allowed a very persistent thirteen-year-old, a black hound dog, and a few stray boards to have the last laugh. This unlikely combination demonstrated that the impossible is indeed possible when faith, diligence, and determination hold their ground in the face of cynicism.

Not all of us will build boats. Not all of us will be Captains or even First Mates. But we all have a work to do – even one as simple as offering encouragement to the one doing the building.

And whatever you do, whether in word or deed,
do it all in the name of the Lord Jesus,
giving thanks to God the Father through Him.

Colossians 3:17
(NIV)

Silver In The Slop

Now it came to pass on a certain day,
that he went into a boat with his disciples:
and he said unto them, Let us go over
unto the other side of the lake.
And they launched forth.
But as they sailed, he fell asleep:
and there came down a storm of wind in the lake;
and they were filled with water,
and were in jeopardy.
And they came to him and awoke him,
saying, Master, master, we perish.
Then he arose, and rebuked the wind
and the raging of the water:
and they ceased, and there was a calm.
And he said unto them,
Where is your faith?
And they being afraid wondered,
saying one to another,
What manner of man is this!
For he commandeth even the winds and water,
and they obey him.

Luke 8:22-25 (KJV)

JONQUILS, WHIPPOORWILLS, AND THE ROLLING STORE

There was nothing quite like spring on Posey Road. Bright jonquils, the first signs of the season, opened their yellow blossoms. My personal whippoorwill returned to her traditional perch in the pine tree outside my window. The baritone voices of the frogs and crickets joined the shrill whippoorwill to create an impressive evening chorus.

This unique evening chorus, however, could not compare to the Rolling Store. A phenomenon unique to our corner of the county, the Rolling Store returned each year at the beginning of spring. Mr. Wright, owner of the country market at the end of Posey Road, seemed to think he would benefit by taking his business on the road. To do that, he converted an old school bus, replacing the seats with shelves and baskets filled with fruit, vegetables, and all the other things you would expect to find in a country store.

Waiting on that noisy bus to squeak down our dirt road was the highlight of the week. Barefoot, toes digging in the sand, I sat at the end of our driveway with my best friend, Deborah. We each held money for a weekend loaf of bread for our Mamas. In addition to the bread money, we each clutched a quarter – payment for gallant promises to rake our yards or clean our rooms.

Deborah and I heard the Rolling Store long before we saw it. Around 11:30 the squeaks grew louder and eventually we saw the old bus appear from a cloud of red dust. As it neared, we jumped up and waved our arms just to be sure Mr. Wright knew we meant business. As soon as the bus stopped and the dust settled, we were aboard.

Those loaves of bread were purchased right away. Mr. Wright knew just what our Mamas wanted and the transaction was completed in a matter of seconds.

Spending those quarters, however, was not to be rushed. Deborah and I made several trips up and down the aisle for inventory purposes. By the fourth trip, Mr. Wright's smile had faded and his foot began to tap impatiently. On the fifth trip, he handed each of us a small brown bag and mentioned that he had to be rolling soon.

Under great pressure, we finally made our purchases. For each of us: one ten-cent candy bar (my favorite was Butterfinger), one large Sweetart for a nickel, five penny chocolate footballs, and five penny pieces of Super Bubble bubble gum – regular and an occasional sour apple.

One simple quarter unquestionably never bought so much happiness!

Throughout the remainder of the day, we nibbled our treasures (the Sweetarts during the Saturday Tarzan movie), discussed our goods (making a few futile attempts at trading), and outlined our purchases for the coming Saturday.

There was nothing quite like spring on Posey Road. The jonquils bloomed. The lightening bugs glowed. My whippoorwill sang.

And on those springs Saturday nights, above the chorus of the crickets and frogs, came the gentle crunch of a Butterfinger candy bar.

Give thanks to the Lord
for He is good.

Psalm 136:1
(NIV)

STUCK IN FORWARD

The Ford Fairlane had seen better days. It looked nice enough – baby blue with a dark blue interior. And what a bargain! It could travel more than a week on one tank of regular gas.

But the right turn signal refused to blink. Mama was forever rolling down the window, extending and bending her arm to indicate a turn. Daddy never bothered with hand signals, figuring other drivers would know he was turning when the car, well, turned. The AM radio played for only about 13 minutes at a time and only then when you hit it firmly over the glove compartment. The car had no air conditioning and each summer Mama, with her fair skin, sported a sunburned left arm from propping it on the open window as she drove. A horrible odor inhabited the Ford Fairlane. Aunt Ola hid a purple boiled egg in the ashtray during an Easter egg hunt one year. No one found the gooey mess until six weeks later when it had a life and odor all its own. We never found any bleach or air freshener powerful enough to destroy six-week-old boiled egg odor.

Despite its shortcomings, the Ford Fairlane did its job. It took us to church each Wednesday and twice on Sunday. It took us to the Crossroads Store during the week for bread and milk. It even took us to school on rainy days when Posey

Road, unpaved and slippery, proved too great an obstacle for our school bus.

Our favorite outing, though, was the Saturday morning trip to town. Town was Newnan, Georgia, a small southern city centered around an historic red brick courthouse. An old clock rested in the tall tower of the courthouse and chimed on the hour.

A trip to town meant stopping at the bank and the Red Dot Grocery Store. Town meant Kessler's Department Store filled with tables of dress material on the first floor and M&Ms at the candy counter on the second floor. Town meant new school shoes every fall at Mr. Hartman's shoe store. Town meant the Bible Bookstore where, I promise, Mama could browse for hours. Town meant automatically bypassing certain stores that Mama labeled too expensive.

The best stores and the prime parking spaces in Newnan were positioned around the Court Square. Standing in front of each parking space were tall gray meters that ate loose change and, in turn, granted you permission to park for an hour or two. Like everyone else, we parked around the Court Square each Saturday. We did, that is, until the day the Ford Fairlane refused to go into reverse.

The Fairlane was parked that day directly in front of the Alamo Theater. Only a few minutes remained on the parking meter. With children and packages safely inside, Mama started the car, placed the gearshift into the proper position, and pressed the gas pedal.

Nothing happened.

The motor hummed but the car sat completely still. Mama shifted gears several times but had the same result. Opening the hood, she saw nothing she understood and closed it with a bang. A few balding men playing checkers on the courthouse steps glanced up in annoyance.

In desperation, Mama finally asked two complete strangers to assist her in pushing the car backward onto the road. Once on Jefferson Street the Ford Fairlane operated perfectly – as long as we moved forward. Mama drove straight home and reported the condition to Daddy. Daddy was not overly concerned.

"Better to get stuck in forward than stuck in reverse," he said.

The car was never repaired. I firmly suspect that the price tag associated with a new transmission was the reason. But we were now aware of the car's limitations. Thus, our Saturday trips to town simply took a different slant.

Parking around the Court Square was impossible. Instead, we drove round and round, up old streets and down back alleys searching for unique places to park – places that required no backward motion from the tired old car.

Inconvenient? Yes. Troublesome? Absolutely. But we quickly discovered a world beyond the Court Square. We saw places we had never seen before! We parked along magnificent tree-lined streets. We parked near brilliant flower gardens outside tall Victorian homes. We parked near railroad tracks and in cul-de-sacs. We parked on a grassy field near the county jail. We parked near the Feed and Seed store where baby chicks lived in a wire pen just inside the door. We once parked near a Texaco Station where the owner kept an alligator named Burt in an old battered Coca-Cola cooler.

We always found a place to park. Always. In fact, parking actually became more of an adventure than a nuisance. The secret was that we always looked forward and were willing to travel new roads.

Daddy traded the Ford Fairlane one autumn day for a green GMC pickup trick with perfect turn signals, a perfect radio, and no boiled egg odor. The truck had a straight shift on the floor and every gear, including reverse, worked flawlessly. Mama was pleased. Daddy was pleased. But, to my horror, we quickly returned to the old way of doing things. Every Saturday we parked on the Court Square, fed the gray parking meters, and saw the same sights every week. Convenient. Uncomplicated. Disgustingly routine. Completely boring.

Reverse is a good thing for Ford Fairlanes and GMC pickup trucks, I have decided. People, though, are meant to move forward – looking ahead, traveling new roads, and discovering the adventure that only the future holds, knowing that whatever our destination, God is already there.

But one thing I do:
Forgetting what is behind
and straining toward what is ahead,
I press on toward the goal to win the prize
for which God has called me heavenward
in Christ Jesus.

Philippians 3:13-14
(NIV)

FREDDY TAKES THE PLUNGE

To most observers it was just a piece of cheap blue plastic. But, to a five-year-old enduring a hot Georgia summer, the little pool was a touch of heaven!

It arrived in a box from the dusty top shelf of Woolworth's Department Store and, once unpacked and filled with air, it transformed my dreary summer into an aquatic adventure. My afternoons were spent leaning against the side of the pool, licking a cherry popsicle, completely at peace with the world.

Home was a large white frame house that once belonged to my grandparents. My father was born in that house, as were his four older brothers and sisters. The house had been built long before the advent of air-conditioning and, even during that blistering summer of 1961, air-conditioning was a luxury we could not afford. So, while the adults swatted flies and cursed the oppressive heat and humidity, I took to the pool.

Life was good, indeed, until the Thursday afternoon I abandoned my spot only briefly in search of one more cherry popsicle. The pool was near the kitchen door so I was gone only a moment.

When I returned, I beheld a sickening sight that, quite possibly, scarred me for life.

Freddy was in my pool!

Unfortunately, Freddy was not a neighbor's child hoping to share my precious pool. Nor was Freddy a tiny puppy in search of a cool drink.

No! Freddy was, instead, 350 pounds of the ugliest, dirtiest, smelliest pig you could possibly imagine. He was probably the biggest, fattest, meanest pig on the farm. And this loathsome creature had somehow escaped the confines of his pen and found his way into the coolest and most inviting spot on a sweltering summer afternoon – my 3 x 5 blue plastic Woolworth's pool!

Furthermore, Freddy was not content to simply sit happily in the water. He wallowed. He rolled upside-down, shifting his rough back from side to side, his stubby legs flailing awkwardly in the air. I watched helplessly as my cool, clear water turned a dirty brown then swooshed over the sides of my beloved pool.

It was unforgivable!

"Mama!" I screamed, pointing to the pool, cherry popsicle trickling down my arm.

Until that moment, Freddy had not noticed me at all, so content was he in his wallowing. But the pig's face froze in panic as he beheld my mother sprinting toward the pool, a broom raised angrily above her head. Stunned and frightened, Freddy struggled to upright himself and flee to the safety of his pen. But as he moved, his hooves struck the bottom and sides of the fragile plastic and, in short order, my beloved pool was completely demolished.

Freddy snorted and ran away, leaving behind a shapeless piece of dirty blue plastic filled with nothing but pig germs and a few drops of muddy water.

My summer was ruined. The season was ending and there were no more blue plastic pools at Woolworth's

Department Store. That signaled the end of my afternoons spent in the cool water. I again found myself inside with the adults, swatting flies and cursing the oppressive heat and humidity.

And it was all the fault of one very dirty, very mean, very insensitive 350-pound pig named Freddy. He had destroyed my pool and violated my personal space.

I never forgave that pig.

Maybe that is why the fresh sausage that winter was especially tasty!

A little while, and the wicked
will be no more;
though you look for them,
they will not be found.

Psalm 37:10
(NIV)

LESSON AT THE MANGER

"Cathy, stop the car!"

The shrill voice of my four-year-old goddaughter Allison blasted the night and drew my attention from the song on the FM. The daughter of my dear friends, Glenda and Gary, Allison and I were constant companions.

It was Christmas Eve and we were traveling home from a last-minute stop at Wal-Mart. We were taking a shortcut when her screech almost stopped my heart.

"What's wrong, Allison?" I asked as I quickly guided the car to the side of the road.

"Look!" she shouted. Her small fingers pointed to an outdoor manger scene. You know the type – cheap plastic with a 40-watt bulb in each figure.

"Cathy, please take me to see it."

"Not now, Allison. We have to get home so Santa Claus can come."

Even as I spoke those words I was disgusted with myself. How could I possibly help teach Allison the true meaning of Christmas with such an attitude?

I drove the car into the driveway of the tiny Church of Christ. Allison jumped out and ran swiftly to the display. As a typical four-year-old, she was not content to simply view the manger -- she had to become part of it!

Allison wandered among the plastic sheep and shepherds and holy family until she touched the plastic baby Jesus. She stood before him, silent, mesmerized.

"Come on, Allison. It's beginning to rain."

Besides, I thought to myself, it is just a gaudy imitation. And there is probably a minister watching who doesn't want a child tipping over his display. Plus, I think I am catching a cold in this drizzle.

"Allison, we've got to go home."

Suddenly, I stopped. In that humbling moment, I reluctantly allowed God to use a four-year-old and a plastic manger scene to speak to me. In an act of genuine, unpretentious love, Allison bent down and kissed the plastic baby Jesus.

"Okay, Cathy, we can go. Now He knows that I love Him."

Jesus said: Unless you become as a little child, you shall not enter the Kingdom of Heaven.

Is it any wonder?

But Jesus called the children to him and said, "Let the little children come to me, and do not hinder them, for the kingdom of God belongs to such as these."

Luke 18:16
(NIV)

TOOTEY-BELLE'S FIRST STEPS

Daddy shivered beneath his old denim coat as he quickly closed the kitchen door behind him. The setting sun made the January evening seem even colder than it actually was. I sat cross-legged by the wood heater, arms outstretched, palms toward the warmth.

"How's Daisy?" I asked.

She was one of my favorite pets – a beautiful Black Angus cow with wide eyes and a gentle personality. She was about to deliver her first calf and, from the beginning, Daisy herself seemed to know things were not going to be easy.

"She's not good," Daddy replied and eventually nodded yes to my noisy pleas to help.

Mama dressed me in several layers of warm clothing, topped by corduroy pants and my stocking cap. Sybil Coggin had knitted that hat for me. While I loved Sybil dearly, I hated that cap and the way it made my hair crackle and stand on end when I pulled it off my head. Mama was adamant, though, taking time to discuss the virtues of stocking caps and the many ailments they would prevent. Knowing I had no choice, I pulled the hat securely over my ears and ran toward the barn.

The quiet of the evening was disturbed only by the "swoosh" of the corduroy and the sound of my own breathing. Swinging open the large doors, I found my father and two neighbors standing over Daisy in the dimly lit barn. She lay on the hay, her wide eyes filled with fear. I squatted beside Daisy and nervously patted her head.

Seconds later, Daisy's body convulsed and, in fear and wonder, I watched a tiny black calf emerge. On his knees, Daddy assisted the animal as it worked its way into the world. Biting my lip, I continued to stroke Daisy, never taking my eyes from the miracle I was witnessing. The calf was out and in a clumsy attempt to stand, suddenly fell to the hay-covered floor. Reaching underneath the calf, Daddy slowly picked the animal off the floor. He brought the calf closer and only when I held her in my arms did I finally see why she was unable to stand. This tiny calf had only three legs! There were two perfectly formed front legs, but only one hind leg.

"Except for that, she's okay," Daddy said as he smiled at me, a curious eight-year-old silently holding a newborn calf in my lap. Awed by the moment, it was a while before I realized that Daisy had lost her struggle for life. Her eyes still open, she lay completely still on her hay-bed. With great sadness, my right hand reached to pet Daisy while I struggled to hold her calf with my other hand. Without speaking, I sat for a very long time, trying to understand what I had just witnessed about the magic and mystery of life and death.

"We'll need a name for her." Daddy's voice interrupted my thoughts.

A name? Yes, we needed a proper name for this small motherless creature with only one back leg.

"Tootey-Belle," Mama spoke up. She had entered the barn quietly just a few moments earlier.

"Tootey-Belle?" Daddy asked, half laughing.

And Tootey-Belle she was. We carried the tiny calf to the house and placed her on a patchwork quilt in front of the wood heater. Mama warmed milk, poured it into a pink plastic baby bottle, and slipped it into Tootey-Belle's mouth. The calf drank eagerly, sucking loudly, a steady stream of white dribbling down her chin. Then, exhausted from her day, she rested quietly by the fire.

The next morning Daddy built a special home for Tootey-Bell in the barn. The pink baby bottle rested nearby until it was replaced with a gray metal bucket with a long nipple near the bottom.

As she grew, Tootey-Belle struggled with her handicap. She learned to stand by cautiously planting her two front feet squarely on the ground then maneuvering her one hind leg properly for balance. Once upright, she wobbled until she steadied herself by leaning against her stall. And she stayed in that spot. Tootey-Belle was afraid to leave the stall and the security of the wall that kept her from falling. I understood her fear and went into the stall to feed her. Daddy, though, wanted her to walk and placed me at the front of the stall with apples and sugar cubes, hoping I could coax the calf toward me. But neither treats nor kind words could persuade the calf to leave her wall.

Tootey-Belle's story spread among the residents of Posey Road and she became quite popular with young and old alike. Neighbors visited often with a treat or an encouraging word, each one secretly hoping to be the one to finally cajole the calf from her pen. Tootey-Belle accepted each gift eagerly but remained in her stall, obviously afraid of falling and unsure of the outside world.

I was growing very impatient with that calf. Daddy, who obviously understood more than I, simply said, "She will walk when it's her time to walk."

At last, on a clear winter afternoon a few days later, when the time was right for Tootey-Belle, she moved slowly to the front of her stall. She nudged the gate open with her nose and looked around cautiously. Watching from a distance, Daddy and I silently cheered for the little calf that finally limped out of her pen. Her head shifted left and right as she surveyed her surroundings, all the while leaning securely against the barn wall. Finally arriving at the barn entrance, Tootey-Belle used the strength of her one back leg to push away from the security of the barn. The calf stood briefly in the barnyard before loosing her balance and falling forward on her front knees.

"She can't do it," I cried.

Daddy caught my arm as I raced toward Tootey-Belle and we continued to watch from afar as the animal struggled to upright herself. Without our help and with no wall to lean against, Tootey-Belle understood that the decision to walk was hers along. Rising awkwardly from the ground, she stood still for a moment and then shifted her legs to balance her body. Gradually she began to move, slowly at first, then faster as she quickly gained confidence.

Tootey-Belle repeated this procedure daily and before long was prancing about the pasture with a rhythm and style all her own. She soon kept pace with all the four-legged creatures. Her fear of falling was replaced with a joyous sense of freedom.

No longer limited to a tiny stall, she was free to explore the acres and acres of land just outside the barn door. She took full advantage of her three good legs to explore the farm. Tootey-Belle walked under the apple trees and ate the delicious sweet fruit. She walked along the pond, pausing whenever she liked to take a cool drink of water. She played happily with the other animals in the pasture.

And each day, for a very long time, the residents Posey Road – people of varying colors, shapes, and sizes – could be found in the Lee pasture, drawn together by a little calf who became famous not for what she lacked, but for what she accomplished.

A longing fulfilled
is sweet to the soul.

Proverbs 13:19
(NIV)

A PIG UNDER PRESSURE

Brunswick Stew. It is a southern standard – a heavenly blending of tomato sauce, vegetables and fresh meat, mostly pork.

It is usually made in the cold weather months. That is when animals are, shall we say, relocated from the pasture to the freezer. It is safer to handle and process meat in the midst of the cold winter temperatures.

But, it was June and the freezer was bare and our empty stomachs could not wait until the next cold snap. It was necessary, therefore, to break with tradition and "transfer" Eunice the pig to the freezer. The deed, seemingly cruel to some, was part of life on a farm. I had watched Eunice grow up and fed her on many occasions. I still knew, however, that her days as a pet were numbered.

Because of our close relationship, I did not choose to share Eunice's final moments. Instead, I waited in the house until called to assist with the next steps. A fire was built and water heated in which to lower the body for preparation. It was a lengthy process that took most of the day; it seemed every longer when you had known your pig personally.

It was late evening by the time Eunice was wrapped and placed in the freezer. We went to bed exhausted, a little sad, but looking forward to the pork chops that would be waiting on the breakfast table.

The next morning, another hot June day, was also Brunswick Stew Day. The stew was traditionally prepared outside, cooked slowly and stirred lovingly in a big black pot over an open fire. The open fire seemed to add just the right touch, blending all the flavors perfectly.

Several steps preceded the black pot and open fire, however. The least enjoyable of which was the preparing of the main staple of the stew – the hog's head. Indeed, the head was to be cooked – boiled to the point that the meat became tender and easy to remove from the bone. This process took several hours over an open fire. It was a curious sight, no doubt, but necessary to the making of Brunswick Stew in the southern tradition.

The heat of that June afternoon, though, did not lend itself to standing over a big black pot and an open fire. Therefore, my mother decided to make use of a timesaving device of the day and placed the hog's head in an extra large pressure cooker. The pressure cooker had belonged to my grandmother and had produced many a meal. Nonetheless, we were quite sure that this was the first hog's head ever to be placed inside this particular cooking apparatus. Mama prepared the head and the cooker, thinking all the while that two hours in a pressure cooker was certainly preferable to five hours over an open fire in the summer heat.

I watched with wide eyes as Mama finalized her preparations and closed the lid on the cooker. It was important to secure the lid because of the steam that would build up during cooking. We each took a step backward as Mama reached over the gadget and turned on the stove eye. I had never seen such a large cooking utensil and was convinced it would never work. Yet, in just a few moments the stove eye turned a familiar red. In a few more moments the cooker began cooking and steam rose from the opening on the top. Mama then placed a stray gray metal piece atop the large pot and the whole contraption began a rhythmic dance on top of the electric stove.

The procedure ended just as we noticed a strange car pulling into the driveway.

"Mrs. Lee? I am Rev. Willis, your new minister."

We were Methodists and they always switched ministers in June and those new ministers had a way of visiting at the worst possible times.

"Since you are the church organist, I wanted to visit you right away. After all, we need to be ready for the service on Sunday, don't we?"

"Certainly," Mama answered. "Come right in and please excuse the house. We've been a little busy here today."

"Well, whatever you are cooking certainly smells delicious," the Reverend said.

I grinned to myself, tickled at the thought of a preacher fancying the aroma of a hog's head.

Mama and the minister seated themselves in the living room and spent the next several minutes discussing preludes, postludes, doxologies, and the like. Rev. Willis seemed nice enough as he paused occasionally to, again, compliment my mother on her cooking. It was just an old family recipe, my mother said, giving no indication that it was Eunice who was rocking away deep within the recesses of a five-gallon pressure cooker.

But, Eunice had the last laugh. It was about this time that the loose lid on the pressure cooker budged to the left, then twisted to the right, and finally blasted toward the ceiling. The lid landed with a crash on the kitchen floor just as Eunice's head flew out of the cooker and rolled into the living room. The object came to a gradual stop about four feet from Mama's chair. Rev. Willis stared at the remains and the remains stared back, sort of, with Eunice's front teeth locked in a vengeful grin.

The pressure cooker was ruined. The electric stove was ruined. The stew was ruined.

Rev. Willis blinked, stammered, and blurted, "What is the meaning of this?"

I looked silently at my Mama.

"Well," she said with peace and poise, "I guess this just proves one thing – if the pressure gets too great, you can really blow your top!"

Now may the Lord of peace himself
give you peace at all times
and in every way.
The Lord be with you.

II Thessalonians 3:16
(NIV)

THE BRA OF MY DREAMS

It wasn't just the bra. It was her attitude concerning the bra.

The Madras School girl's restroom was packed with fourth graders washing up after morning recess. I was elbowing my way through the crowd when Betsy Fowler's shrill voice rang above the chatter.

"Well, look at this. My bra strap just won't stay in place."

An uneasy silence enveloped the Madras School girl's restroom. Betsy shoved a very obvious white strap underneath the shoulder of her sleeveless pink and white polka-dot shirtwaist dress and smiled smugly.

I hated her at that moment.

It didn't matter that being the largest girl in the class she would naturally be the first to need a bra. It didn't matter that as an only child Betsy was constantly showered with gifts from adoring parents. All that mattered was that Betsy Fowler was the first girl in the Madras School fourth grade to wear a bra and she had succeeded in making the rest of us aware of that fact. Though it was not discussed openly, I firmly believe that, right then, every girl in that restroom silently vowed to secure a bra before sundown. Me included.

Needless to say, I concentrated little on science and arithmetic the rest of that Monday afternoon. I wanted a bra in the worst way and by the time the final bell rang, it was an obsession. I rode the bus home in silence, daydreaming of the scene that would surely unfold when I arrived home. I would walk up to Mama and calmly announce: "Mother . . . it is time. I must have a bra."

She would take me in her arms, shower me with kisses while shedding a bucket of maternal tears over how quickly I had grown up. Together we would drive to town where, with great ceremony, we would choose the perfect bra. It would be pure white, decorated with lace and a tiny pink flower adorning the front. In my fantasy, this would be a special day my mother and I would recall fondly for the rest of our lives.

As the bus stopped, I jumped off and raced up the driveway. Mama stood at the kitchen sink and, my fantasy abruptly abandoned, I blurted, "Betsy Fowler has a bra and I've just got to get one!"

Mama slowly dried her hands. She took one step back and looked at me squarely for several agonizing seconds before muttering five horrible little words: "You don't need a bra!"

Need? Who said anything about need? It never dawned on me that I *needed* a bra. The situation was simple – Betsy Fowler had a bra and, therefore, I wanted one.

I didn't care about the job a bra performed. I was not suffering from "cleavage envy" nor did I want anything to put into the bra. I simply wanted a bra. Immediately! I wanted to stand in the Madras School girl's restroom and push a lacy white bra strap underneath the shoulder of a sleeveless dress.

The look on Mama's face, though, told me that she simply did not understand my situation. Furthermore, she had no intention of showering me with kisses, shedding maternal tears, or driving me to town for a precious white bra decorated with lace and a pink flower.

My fantasy died right there in the kitchen on Posey Road.

Life was brutal. By suppertime I was convinced that the next morning I would be the only fourth grade girl attending Madras School bra-less. Horrified, I did what any other normal fourth grade child would do – I nagged, I pestered, I whined. I accused my mother of not loving me, of not caring about my reputation nor my general well being. I compared her unfavorably to mothers of my classmates. I brooded and sulked while murmuring Betsy Fowler's name under my breath. I was obnoxious and bratty. But I was persistent and when I climbed into bed on Thursday night, my blessed and beleaguered mother surrendered.

"I will pick you up after school tomorrow and we will go to town and buy you a trainer."

A TRAINER?

I began to worry. A trainer? What was a trainer? Was it a bra? If so, was it lacy and white? Did it have a pink flower on the front? And furthermore, was I ready for a trainer? I didn't know training was involved in this particular growth process. Didn't the contents of a bra just grow naturally? What was I supposed to train them to do? And what if I trained them wrong? After all, I was only nine years old and, without realizing it, I could disfigure myself for life. Training? This was a lot of responsibility to place on a fourth grader.

I hardly slept at all.

****

True to her word, Mama was waiting for me when the final bell rang. My stomach hurt and I was afraid I would throw up long before we walked into Kessler's on the Court Square in Newnan.

Inside, we met a tall lady with gray hair and tiny glasses perched on the end of her nose.

"We've come to purchase a bra," Mama announced. Over the top of her glasses the gray-haired lady looked at me with the same expression my mother had given me earlier in the week. She didn't say those five little words, but I knew she was thinking them.

"I think we need a trainer," she said. My stomach began to hurt again.

Taking a second look at me, she walked toward a rack holding small pastel boxes. She opened a blue box and held up a trainer. My stomach relaxed and I began breathing normally. It was a bra – and it was perfect! It was a brilliant white. Lace decorated the bottom and, to my delight, a petite pink flower sat front and center. Trainer or not, it was the bra of my dreams. Surely Betsy Fowler had no finer bra.

"We'll take it," Mama announced. I left the store without saying a word but, as I walked toward the door, I was sure everyone was staring at me, fully aware that a bra rested inside my brown shopping bag.

In the safety of my own room, I pulled the bra from the blue box. What next? From what I understood, there were two schools of thought regarding the proper way to put on a bra. I decided to go with the "fasten in the front then twist to the back" technique. That is what Mama did so it had to be correct. No one in our family had ever attempted the "direct back-hook" approach, whereby you placed the bra over your arms then contorted and twisted your hands behind you to fasten the hooks directly in the back.

As I began my "fasten in the front then twist to the back" maneuver, a major problem was immediately evident. The ends of the bra did not meet. Yes, I was a chubby child and the lady at Kessler's had obviously misjudged my circumference. I needed at least another two inches of material to allow the hooks to connect. But, in my stubborn determination to place that bra on my body, I had a stroke of brilliance!

My mother's sewing basket was filled with large safety pins. I would fasten a safety pin to one side of the bra, then interlock the necessary number of pins to grasp the opposite side. It would create a sort of chain effect that would connect the two sides of the bra.

The idea was a good one until I began the "twist to the back" motion. Those safety pins had no intention of sliding smoothly around my middle. Instead, they fought back, popping open and sticking painful little holes in my midriff.

Defeated, I turned to Mama.

"It doesn't fit," I whispered, almost in tears.

We returned to Kessler's the next morning where the tall lady looked over her glasses, found a different blue box, and sent me on my way.

This bra business was unquestionably more complicated than I had initially foreseen. Nevertheless, my second bra was a better fit. I am proud to say that at approximately 3:00 p.m. on that weekend afternoon, closure was achieved!

Emotionally exhausted, I placed the bra safely inside my top drawer where it would remain until I dressed for school Monday morning. I slept peacefully that night, quite happy with myself for getting exactly what I wanted.

* * * * * * * *

Monday morning. I awoke before the alarm sounded. My dress had been carefully chosen – pale yellow tulips on a blue background. It was sleeveless, of course, thus allowing my bra strap to make an appearance at a strategic moment during the school day. The garment felt quite strange but I was confident it would feel more natural the longer I wore it. Climbing aboard the school bus, I felt like a true woman of the world. With one meager appearance of a simple bra strap, I planned to personally wipe that smug look off the face of Miss Betsy Fowler.

Arithmetic – definitely not my favorite subject -- was my first class that day. To my surprise, I knew the answer to the first question the teacher asked. Raising my hand enthusiastically I discovered, to my horror, that my bra went with it!

Instead of staying in its intended location, the garment slithered up my chest and crept rapidly toward my neck. I instantly lowered my hand and turned crimson with embarrassment. Were bras supposed to do this? Hoping no one was watching, I hunched over my desk, discreetly tugging and yanking, trying desperately to return the bra to its proper position.

As I made my final adjustments, the teacher called my name.

"Cathy, could you come to the board and show us how to work this problem."

I walked slowly to the front of the room, selected a piece of chalk, and lifted my arm to write numbers on the blackboard. As I did, the bra lurched upward. It climbed toward my throat, twisting and pinching as it moved. Had some demon, intent on ruining my life, gained control of this innocent garment? The bra kept crawling higher and higher until it seemed ready to shoot through the neck of my dress. I was sure everyone in the class could see an abnormal wrinkle crisscrossing my chest. Holding me in its tight grip, the wicked combination of elastic and lace threatened my dignity and bound upper chest until I could barely breathe.

Excusing myself quickly, I ran to the bathroom. I was no longer interested in showing my strap to Betsy Fowler and the other girls in my fourth grade class. I was interested in pure, basic survival.

My mind raced as I jerked the bra back into place. What could I do with this cursed object? I had no purse. I couldn't just stuff it into one of my books. Surely one of the boys in class would find it and I would die from the resulting ridicule. I couldn't throw the bra away – Mama would never let me hear the end of it. I couldn't call home sick and listen to my Mama's "I told you so" the rest of the day.

There was no alternative. I had to wear the horrible contraption until the end of the day. I could do it, I told myself, as long as I didn't move my arms. Thus, I spent the rest of the day walking like a short robot programmed to keep my arms glued tightly to my side.

It was one of the longest days of my life.

I stepped off the bus that afternoon completely humiliated. Walking silently to my room, I removed that cursed garment and stuffed it in the back corner of my dresser drawer. I prayed I would never see it again.

Mama never mentioned the bra again. Neither did I. But, when the time was right and I *needed* one, we returned to Kessler's and bought a suitable bra for me. Because I then possessed the necessary anatomical components, the bra stayed easily in place. I could move my hands and arms in any direction without fear of "bra repositioning."

Oh, the agony I could have avoided if I had simply listened to my Mama! She knew best, but instead of heeding her wise counsel, I was controlled by my childish impatience. As a consequence, I suffered one of the worst days of my life.

I wish I could say that the training bra episode taught me, once and for all, to live in harmony with my needs instead of my wants. God has promised to meet my *needs* but, after all these years, I still question why he doesn't fulfill my *wants,* especially when those wants seem so sensible to me. My greatest difficulties arise when I am so bound by my wants that I fail to cherish the many blessings God has already brought into my life. Perhaps, as in the case of my white lace training bra, God will give me just what I want – but only when I am mature enough to receive it.

I have worn many bras since that horrible day at Madras School so long ago. I have worn underwires and cross-your-hearts. I have worn two-hookers, four-hookers, back-hookers and front-hookers. I have worn T-backs, U-backs, posture bras and sports bras. I have worn strapless bras, bras with comfort straps, and bras with frayed straps held together with a few strategically placed safety pins. I've worn white bras, black bras, ivory bras, and once, on a dare, a leopard skin bra. Occasionally, I still wear a bra with a tiny pink flower on the front.

Ironically, there are now many times I don't *want* to wear a bra at all, but nowadays I really *need* one.

I can still recall clearly that awful day in the fourth grade. Would I have been more patient had I known just how many bras were in my future? Probably not. I was controlled completely by my wants. My needs were not an issue. And though quite a few years have passed since I was in the fourth grade, I still struggle with this same problem.

It is a hard thing to realize that I do not always know what is best for me. Mama knew best in the fourth grade. God knows best today and everyday.

Grant me the wisdom I need, O Lord, to praise you for meeting my needs – and to trust Your wisdom when it comes to controlling my wants.

For I have learned to be content in whatever circumstances I am. I know how to get along with humble means, and I also know how to live in prosperity; in any and every circumstance I have learned the secret of being filled and going hungry, both of having abundance and suffering need. I can do all things through Him who strengthens me . . . . And my God shall supply all your NEEDS according to His riches in glory in Christ Jesus. Now to our God and Father be the glory forever and ever. Amen.

Selection from Philippians 4:11-20
(New American Standard)

HIS FAMILY TREE

As the wind blew and the cold rain stung his face, the little boy said to himself, "It will never make it through the night. It's tiny and fragile and alone."

With very little effort, the boy took hold of the small seedling and pulled gently. The wet ground easily surrendered the tiny tree and with one swift motion, the little boy thrust it into his backpack.

"There," he said. "I'll plant it in my yard and take care of it myself."

And he did just that. As the sun shone brightly the next morning, the little boy jumped out of bed, threw on his old clothes, and ran to the front yard. He silently surveyed the yard around the gray house on 26th Street searching for the perfect place. Near the back porch? Not suitable. Next to the garage? No. Maybe next to the chicken coup. Certainly not.

The boy quietly marched around the house a second time before finally dropping to his knees, digging a hole, and planting the small seedling next to the front porch facing the street. He stepped back and looked.

"It still seems tiny and fragile and alone," he thought. "But it has me and I will take care of it."

And he did just that. He watered the tree when the ground was dry and pulled menacing weeds away from the trunk. When Christmas came, the small cedar was strong enough to provide a home for a tiny string of twinkling white lights. Hugged by the bright sparkles, the tree did not appear so tiny and fragile and alone. On the contrary, it added light and warmth to the house on 26th Street.

As the little boy grew, so did the tree. The limbs gave shade to the boy and his friends as they laughed and played and shared secrets. The ground underneath gave cool refuge as the boy read and studied and thought deep boyhood thoughts. Under the tree he dreamed of growing up and growing old and it made him feel happy and sad at the same time.

When the next Christmas came, the cedar provided a home for two strings of twinkling white lights. More lights were added each Christmas until no one could reach the top of the tree, not even with the tallest ladder.

Amazingly, no one could remember when the tree was tiny and fragile and alone. No one except the boy who quickly grew into a young man who went away to school in another town. But he smiled every time he drove home to the gray house on 26th Street because the tree stood tall to welcome him.

The tree provided a sanctuary for the young man during his rare days at home. The limbs gave shade to him. The ground underneath gave cool refuge as the young man read and studied and thought deep college thoughts. Under the tree he dreamed of growing up and growing old and it made him feel happy and sad at the same time.

The day arrived when the young man left the gray house on 26th Street for the last time. His father died and his mother moved to the other side of town, into a small apartment with no trees in the front yard.

Another family bought the house on 26th Street and painted it a brilliant yellow. Knowing his home no longer stood on 26th Street, he built a new home in a distant city.

The years quickly passed and, one autumn day, the man and his wife found themselves in his hometown. His wife said, "Show me where you lived as a little boy."

The man paused thoughtfully, then turned onto 26th Street. He drove slowly, studying the changes that reflected a twenty-five year absence. He parked the car along the familiar street and opened the door. Taking his wife's hand, he walked slowly toward the house.

Someone had painted over the yellow and the house was now a dull white with black shutters. The garage was gone. The chicken coup was gone. The trees and flowers in the back yard were gone.

But *his* tree was there – a tall, stately cedar majestically guarding the front porch of the house on 26th Street.

He beheld the tree, slowly surveying its broad trunk, its curling limbs, and its grand height. Studying the tree, the man marveled at how quickly he had grown up and grown old and he felt happy and sad at the same time.

Just then, deep within the man a little boy stirred, and the man smiled, because just for a moment he was home.

And he squeezed his wife's hand and gently said, "Come on. Let me tell you about that tree."

He presented another parable to them, saying,
"The kingdom of heaven is like a mustard seed,
which a man took and sowed in his field;
and this is smaller than all other seeds;
but when it is full grown,
it is larger than the garden plants,
and becomes a tree,
so that the birds of the air
come and nest in its branches."

Matthew 13:31-32
(New American Standard)

HOLDING DADDY'S HAND

"No, I'm not going into the water."

I believed her, this five-year-old standing stubbornly in the sand, arms crossed, her chubby legs protruding from a yellow swimsuit with ruffles across the bottom.

"She's never seen the ocean before," her father explained, somewhat embarrassed. "I guess she's a little scared."

I could hardly blame her. It was not the best day for a beach outing. Storms would be rolling in later that day and the wind was already blowing steadily. Instead of a calm blue, the water was colored a murky green from the seaweed that washed ashore. The waves were high and crashed wildly onto the beach, leaving behind a dirty foam that snaked across the wet sand.

A brave few remained in the water but I opted for the security of a sand chair and a romance novel, perfectly content until the five-year-old caught my eye.

"Please, Stacy, this is our last day here and you haven't gone into the water at all."

They would leave the next day for their home in Tennessee and Stacy might not see the ocean again for a very long time.

"No, Daddy," she said. "The water is too big. I'm afraid."

And she resumed the construction of the most lopsided sandcastle I had ever seen. She spent her time shoveling and patting sand, digging moats and fashioning turrets. Occasionally she would pause and stare at the ocean as if struggling to find the courage to step into the water.

"Do you want to play in the waves?" her father pleaded again.

"I'm still afraid, Daddy."

Moving away from the sandcastle, Stacy collected seashells in a pink plastic bucket. She played on the beach, covering her feet with sand, patting it firmly, and then giggling aloud as the sand collapsed when she pulled her feet free. She walked up and down the beach laughing and singing, dancing and exploring, pausing once or twice to study the movement of the water. Her father watched her closely.

Suddenly she turned and called to him. "Will you hold my hand, Daddy? Will you hold it real tight and not let go?"

Her father was up in an instant, dusting sand off him as he walked toward his daughter.

"I promise," he said as he reached down, wrapping his fingers tightly around hers. Hand-in-hand they walked toward the ocean.

Stacy stepped slowly, pausing once to dig her toes into the cool, damp sand. She laughed nervously as the edge of the frothy water first tickled her toes. When the water covered her ankles, she glanced anxiously at her father. Assured of his presence, Stacy slowly turned back toward the waves, confidently planting one foot in front of the other until she stood waist-deep in the water. Picking her up, Stacy's father carried her deeper into the ocean, clutching her tightly in his strong, loving arms. Linking her arms around his neck, the two bounced and bobbed joyously on the waves. They laughed aloud as the salty water splashed their faces and dripped from their noses.

As the storm approached, the waves grew stronger. The two stood resolute, though, often pushed backward by the force but never tumbling into the water. Holding her all the while, Stacy and her father played joyously until the rains came. As I gathered my things and ran for shelter, the sounds of their laughter still rang above the wind and the waves.

I have faced waves of my own since that day on the beach – waves of fear, waves of grief, waves of uncertainty and self-doubt. Many waves have struck forcefully, threatening to drown my spirit and my faith. But when those inevitable waves threaten, I recall a five-year-old facing the ocean for the very first time.

Then, taking my lead from Stacy, I stand firm, face the waves head-on, and hold a little tighter to my Father.

So do not fear, for I am with you;
Do not be dismayed, for I am your God.
I will strengthen you and help you;
I will uphold you with my victorious right hand.

Isaiah 41:10
(RSV)

BRIGHT LIGHTS ON DARK NIGHTS

From the dirt road we turned onto a secluded pathway choked with rocks and tall weeds. The old house that once stood proudly at the end of the trail had burned years before. Only a lonely chimney stood strangely silhouetted against the night sky.

With the car lights off, the darkness seemed thick and sinister. The night was quiet, disturbed by only a few rustling leaves and soft chorus of distant crickets. We quickly agreed that this was the perfect place – remote, quiet, and very dark.

Leaning against the side of his car, Gene opened a brown paper bag and reached carefully inside. He handed one small bundle to his wife, Mimi, and gave the second to me. The third he kept for himself. As the cellophane crackled loudly, we eagerly unwrapped our Little Debbie raisin cakes. Gene opened a quart of cold chocolate milk. There was nothing to do but wait.

We talked as we waited, building what we knew would be a lasting friendship. Thought we had known each other only a few weeks, our friendship had developed quickly and naturally.

We were family, we decided, even though we had only recently met.

Our words began to flow freely as Gene passed around the chocolate milk. We talked of dogs and horses and our favorite movies. We talked of our private longings and our dreams for the future. We shared funny stories as the sounds of joyful laughter danced across the darkness. We talked of angels and miracles and of God's special blessings in our lives. And, we recalled dark moments when life seemed grim and God far too distant.

For a moment, the dark reminded me all too clearly of some of those distressing moments. In an instant, the night turned frightening and overwhelming.

As I fought the temptation to drive swiftly back to the city, a bright light suddenly exploded in the evening sky. Streaking across the darkness for only a second, the bright flash was brilliant and well worth our time and the price of three Little Debbie raisin cakes. My fear of the darkness vanished with the beginning of this summer meteor shower.

Within moments the sky erupted with stars shooting across the heavens. The meteors were beautiful but completely unpredictable. We never knew when or where they would next appear. At times the lights erupted in quick succession. Then, without warning, the sky would suddenly grow still and somber. At other times, just when we felt the show had surely ended, a beam would again burst into view and skip across the heavens. The most dazzling lights danced directly above us. So, we spent most of the evening stretching our necks skyward, afraid that if we watched only the distant horizon, we would miss the most brilliant meteors altogether.

Our light show continued for several hours, far longer than the raisin cakes and chocolate milk. We smiled and clapped and cheered. We laughed out loud like little children discovering something wonderful for the very first time. Our friendship grew with each moment of that miraculous evening. Against a canopy of darkness, God had fashioned a celestial show of fireworks perfectly choreographed to the gentle song of the crickets.

Eventually the meteors subsided and the night grew dark again. I was no longer anxious, though. I smiled to myself, thankful for the beauty of the light, the gift of friendship, and the certainty of God's presence.

Even though the darkness returned, I saw some things in a new light.

When we look heavenward with expectant hearts, we will never be disappointed. God is always near. If we fail to see Him, perhaps it is because we are looking at a distant horizon and not directly above us.

I am especially confident, and this is the most important part, that the light of God's presence has illuminated even my darkest moments. And doesn't light always shine its brightest in the deepest darkness?

When Jesus spoke to the people, He said,
"I am the light of the world.
Whoever follows me will never
walk in darkness,
but will have the light of life."

John 8:12
(NIV)

A GOOD DOSE OF VICTORY

"Take your pick," Jennifer said as she pointed to a large cardboard box in the corner of her basement.

Jennifer was my best friend. Jennifer's best friend (other than me and, I suppose, her husband, Dick) was Scarlett, a beautiful black and white English Springer Spaniel who had just given birth to nine tiny puppies. Most were black and white, just like their mother. A few, however, bore the liver and white colors of their father.

All were beautiful, of course. But one in particular caught my eye. A liver and white male in the center of this bundle of brand new canines worked feverishly to reach Scarlett and her ample supply of mother's milk. Separating the pile of puppies, I instinctively reached for this tiny dog and held him close to my chest. I stroked him and, in turn, he nuzzled my neck with his wet nose. Then, placing his head underneath my chin, he quietly fell asleep.

Ah, yes, this was my dog. In an instant, we bonded and became a family.

"What about a name?" Jennifer inquired.

Glancing at the puppy, I noticed an unusual V-shaped marking just where the liver and white colors converged on the back of his tiny neck.

"V is for Victory," I said. "It is a perfect name for a perfect dog."

Unusual, yes, but Victory was the perfect name for this dog. You see, this puppy was born on January 12, 1993 at 7:30 p.m., exactly one year to the minute since my husband, Jerry, had passed away. On the AKC papers he was listed officially as "Jerry's January Victory." To me, he is just plain Victory, the wonder dog.

Now, do I believe this dog is some strange reincarnation of my husband? Absolutely not! But in our very last conversation, Jerry and I discussed puppies. Jerry had recently spent a good deal of time in the hospital and the house was very lonely without him.

"I want someone warm and cuddly to come home to," I told him that afternoon of January 12, 1992.

"Well," he joked, "I would rather you find a puppy than another man! So, let us find you a puppy and let us do it quickly."

Jerry died later that same night and, needless to say, finding a new puppy was not a priority. Simple survival during a time of intense grief was my main concern.

But when Jennifer and her husband, Dick, offered me one of Scarlett's puppies, I felt the time was right to share my home with someone else, even a four-legged someone else.

The six weeks Victory remained with his mother seemed an eternity. On the first possible day, I went to their home complete with a large bag filled with colorful dog toys and a new doggie bed. I was quite anxious to take Victory to his new home. He made the transition quite easily. On those first nights, I let the tiny puppy snuggle in the bed with me before placing him in his own bed on the floor next to mine.

Victory grew so quickly! One day he was a tiny creature with tightly closed eyes; the next, a rambunctious puppy; and the next, a noble adult dog. Throughout each stage of growth, he remained a loving and playful roommate.

One of my greatest joys was coming home from work to someone warm and loving who was continually happy to see me. We spent many evenings playing in front of the fireplace. His favorite toy was a hideous green piece of plastic resembling a large stalk of celery. I threw it across the room and he fetched perfectly. He never quite understood that he was to return it and drop it into my hand, so we played a tug-of-war with the toy until, exhausted, he lay down beside me in front of the fire.

Victory was my shadow. If I played the piano, he rested quietly under the bench. If I worked on my computer, he sat next to my feet. His favorite activity, by far, was simply crawling into my lap and resting patiently while I petted him tenderly. Even through my days overflowing with grief, I felt my spirit lifting a bit. This special dog made an inroad into my heart that helped me believe I could actually love something again. Victory reminded me of the value of touch, too, as he jumped into my arms and licked my face. It felt wonderful to, once again, touch another living creature who so willingly gave love to me.

I am proud to say that Victory is alive and well and still a very important part of my life. After our recent move to South Carolina, he was able to escape the confines of a fenced yard in a very busy Atlanta neighborhood. He now spends his days roaming the woods, running, playing, and simply being a dog.

Victory still works me into his busy schedule, however. Jumping with excitement, he greets my car as soon as it enters the driveway. More often than not, he climbs into the car with me before I am able to gather my things and exit the vehicle. Victory walks me to my door and, once I am inside, he watches me through the sliding glass door. I usually find a few moments to spend "quality time" with him before being distracted by silly things such cooking dinner, cleaning house, talking to friends on the phone, or writing a book.

Many evenings I sit on the front porch and watch the sunset. Walking behind me, Victory nuzzles his head next to me, forcing me to drape my arm over the V-marking on the back of his neck. Quite content, he sits with me as long as I remain on the porch. And on those inevitable days when loneliness prevails and my emotions are close to the surface, he seems to understand and seeks to comfort me in his own way. He tilts his head as if to say, "I'll be glad to listen if you want to talk." At least that is what this dog owner reads into his expression. I firmly believe that Victory would do anything within his power to make me feel better at those moments.

Victory never fails to show me unconditional love and acts as though I am the most wonderful person he has ever met. Is it possible that I will ever find a man who can meet the standards Victory has set for a relationship in my life?

It is good to know that when the frustrations are many and the rewards are few, I can sit quietly on my porch and be comforted by a good dose of Victory.

Dear Lord, please help me be the person my dog thinks I am!

But who teaches us more
than the beasts of the earth,
and makes us wiser than the birds of the heavens?

Job 35:11
(New American Standard)

SINGLE IS . . . . .

Authors Note:

Single at age 35. That was not what I planned for my life, but that was my circumstance after Jerry's death in 1992. To be bluntly honest, I didn't like it. And I'm not thrilled with it now. I had a great marriage, a loving husband, and plans for us to grow old together. I still want my marriage back, but that cannot be.

Therefore, one night I decided I needed an attitude adjustment and I compiled the following list of the positive aspects of being single. And, of course, there are positive aspects. Whenever I share my list with singles groups, they laugh, but they also have their own thoughts to add.

Creating this list did not completely change my perspective, but reading it from time to time reminds me to look for the silver in the slop!

Read my list. Then, whether you are married, single, or facing any difficult situation in your life, make a list of the positive things in your own life and give thanks to God for his blessings!

BEING SINGLE MEANS. . . .

- I can eat ice cream (or, in my case, low-fat frozen yogurt), right out of the container.
- I can listen to Christmas music in July.
- I can leave the house cluttered and no one will complain.
- I can leave the house spotless and no one will mess it up.
- The phone always rings for me.
- I can leave leftovers in the refrigerator and no one else eats them.
- I can sing out loud and no one giggles.
- I can use all the closets for my clothes.
- All the drawer space is mine.
- I never have to buy bananas.
- The toilet paper always goes over the top of the roll.
- The toilet seat is always down.
- I can walk around in my pajamas whenever I want.
- I can take long showers and use up all the hot water.
- I don't have to cook if I don't want to.
- I can belch out loud without having to say, "Excuse me."
- I have a lot less laundry to do.
- I can arrange the furniture any way I want.
- I can sleep all night with the TV on.
- I don't have to spray air freshener in the bathroom after I have been in there a really long time.

- I never have to invite people I don't like over for dinner.
- No one tells me I should eat liver once a week.
- I can watch whatever I want on TV.
- I don't have to talk to anyone in the evenings if I don't want to.
- No one drinks all the orange juice and then puts the empty container back into the refrigerator.
- I can spend my money however I wish.
- I make my own plans.
- No one flushes the toilet and scalds my backside while I am taking a shower.
- No one reads the Sunday paper before I do.
- No one punches me if I snore at night – although I am quite confident I do not snore! (Well, maybe just a little when I am a tad congested.)

Where can I go from your Spirit?
Where can I flee from your presence?
If I go up to the heavens, you are there;
if I make my bed in the depths, you are there.
If I rise on the wings of the dawn,
if I settle on the far side of the sea,
even there your hand will guide me,
your right hand will hold me fast.

Psalm 139:7-10
(NIV)

DOCTOR DADDY

Whatever your ailment, Daddy believed he could cure it in one of three ways:

1. Hot Salty Water
2. Vicks VapoRub
3. Epsom Salt

Doctors were only good for taking your money, he believed. So, unless blood was pouring uncontrollably from an open wound, we were treated with one of the aforementioned home remedies.

Unfortunately, I was prone to tonsillitis as a child. The remedy? Gargle three times per day with hot salty water.

Chest cold or pneumonia? Apply a large glob of Vicks VapoRub to your chest and rub vigorously. Next, warm a hand towel on top of the wood heater and place it over your chest. The smell of camphor and menthol filled the room. I am not sure whether I was actually cured by this procedure or I just pretended to be better to escape the smell.

For a twisted limb, mashed finger, or serious cut, fill a pan with warm water and Epsom salt. Soak the injury for thirty minutes three times per day. Sooner or later our aches and pains would subside and Daddy would walk around with an "I told you so" smirk on his face.

During my 16th year I contracted an unusually stubborn case of tonsillitis. My throat turned white with infection and I ran a high fever for several days. My tonsils were swollen and irritated. Swallowing was an agonizing excursion into the world of pain. Worst of all, I missed several days of school which, quite frankly, interfered with my 16-year-old social life. Daddy prescribed the hot salty water remedy but after four days, my throat was still inflamed. Mama added the Vicks VapoRub treatment for good measure, but my tonsillitis continued.

Tired of being sick, I growled, "When I grow up I will go to a real doctor when I am sick. He will give me real medicine for a real recovery!"

Mama finally took me to the doctor who gave me antibiotics that cured me within a few days. Daddy, however, still believed the gargling had actually done the trick.

* * * * * * *

Fast forward to 1997. At her invitation, I was studying voice with an excellent instructor, June Kessler Cowin. She heard potential in my singing and I was both surprised and delighted! I had always wanted to sing but never felt I had the ability. Nevertheless, I finally trusted her instinct and was pleased to be working with her. I knew far less than her other students and, therefore, worked extra hard each week. Before long, my lack of confidence was replaced with a genuine joy of performance.

One day, however, my instructor uttered one small word that struck fear in my heart: *RECITAL.* Each year her students performed in the White Hall Auditorium at Emory University. Standing center stage with only an accompanist and a grand piano, there was no room for error.

I studied in earnest. Memorization was a requirement, but this memorization was not limited to words alone. I worked for hours to perfect my breathing, my enunciation, my expression and delivery. Because I was singing several songs in foreign languages, I had to consider the pronunciation of each word in its proper dialect. I was learning that singing correctly was hard work. At the same time, though, it was exhilarating because I was challenging myself, learning something completely new, and realizing a dream I had long held. I also got to wear a really cute dress for the performance!

As the recital date drew near, I worked even longer hours until the morning I noticed a slight tickle in my throat. By the end of the day the tickle was a dull pain. By the following day, it felt as though someone had set fire to my sinuses, head, and throat. I developed a deep cough that burned my raw throat, irritating it further. The following day my voice failed and I could barely speak above a whisper.

My recital was six days away.

In desperation I called my Ear, Nose, and Throat Specialist. He loaded me down with antibiotics, decongestants, nasal sprays, and cough syrup. He insisted that I rest and not speak any more than was absolutely necessary. (This was especially difficult for me.)

My voice made some improvement, but each time I tried to practice my music, the sound would quickly vanish. My instructor fixed me hot tea with lemon and worried about the approaching date.

In the midst of this crisis, Daddy called one day. Upon hearing my voice, he told me to immediately get up and gargle with hot salty water. And, did I have any Vicks VapoRub in the house for the rattling in my chest?

"Daddy," I screeched with my scratchy throat, "my doctor is one of the most distinguished ear, nose, and throat specialists in Atlanta. I am sure he has some state-of-the-art medication that will soothe my cough and restore my voice before my recital. I have come a long way since my childhood on Posey Road. I will not resort to an old home remedy when I have such a brilliant doctor at my disposal."

Daddy laughed quietly and hung up the phone.

I returned to my doctor the next day and in a whisper desperately begged for help. My recital was only two days away.

"Well, it is time to give you the Singer's Treatment," he said, as he scribbled in his chart and pulled two long needles from a drawer. He gave me one shot -- a steroid that would go to work immediately to rid my body of the infection it was fighting. Then he gave me a second shot, another steroid, a time-released medication that would continue to fight my illness over the next several days. He prescribed more decongestants and furnished another dose of cough syrup to sooth my tender throat.

"Go home and rest, keep quiet, and your voice will be ready for you to sing on Saturday," he promised.

I walked toward the door, feeling quite proud that I had been given the "Singer's Treatment" by my very capable physician. Thanks to his knowledge and training, the show would go on!

As I gathered my things and prepared to leave, my doctor offered me one last bit of advice that will probably haunt me forever.

"By the way, it would be a good idea if you would gargle three times a day with hot salty water."

Listen, my son, to your father's instruction
and do not forsake your mother's teaching.
They will be a garland to grace your head
and a chain to adorn your neck.

Proverbs 1:8-9
(NIV)

PUTTING ON THE RITZ

"The Ritz Carlton? Well, maybe I can adjust my schedule."

The rat! For several weeks I had been begging Jennifer to go to the beach with me but a variety of scheduling conflicts kept her close to home. So, being an independent woman of the world, I decided to go by myself. *I've been to college and I hold a steady job,* I thought, *I certainly can go to the beach by myself.*

I called my travel agent with my criteria: I wanted to practically roll out of the bed and onto the beach. And I wanted something relatively close. I didn't want to spend my entire vacation driving to and from my destination.

Within the hour my travel agent called back. "Have I got a deal for you," she practically shouted with excitement. "In fact, if you don't take this, I will."

The Ritz Carlton, Amelia Island, Florida. They were offering a special rate of $159 per night for a suite that normally rented for $650 per night. The Ritz Carlton! I had never visited a Ritz before but I knew of their reputation for being the ultimate in pampering and luxury.

"Book it!" I told my travel agent.

Next, I called Jennifer to gloat. She was my best friend, a fellow PW (Preacher's Wife), with a temperament so like mine it was frightening. Most people thought we were sisters because of our similar looks and personality. Of course, because I had no gray hair, people naturally thought I was the younger sister.

Our husbands pastored neighboring United Methodist Churches in Cherokee County, Georgia. Therefore, we saw each other often at community and church events. We quickly became close friends. Jennifer was a teacher, having a long summer vacation, so it seemed sensible that she could accompany me to the beach. But her summer calendar filled quickly that year. It seemed that she had no time for pitiful little me -- until I mentioned The Ritz Carlton. Like me, she only knew of the Ritz by reputation and couldn't pass up the chance to spend a few days in this luxury resort.

In short, Jennifer somehow changed her plans and on a hot July afternoon, these two preacher's wives from Cherokee County turned toward the beach. Over the six-hour drive we talked and laughed like two teenagers at a slumber party. We sang with the radio and even played word games to pass the time.

As we neared the island, however, we began to think seriously about something important to both of us – snacks! We were on vacation; everyone knows calories do not count while you are on vacation. We had no idea what edibles the hotel would offer so we made a quick stop at a convenience store for the basics:

- ✓ Two cases of Caffeine-Free Diet Coke
- ✓ Double Stuff Oreos
- ✓ Cheese and Crackers
- ✓ Cherry Pop Tarts for Breakfast
- ✓ One Bag of Almond Joy Candy Bars
- ✓ An oversize bag of bright orange cheese puffs
- ✓ And one disposable razor because Jennifer had forgotten to shave her legs

In our old shorts and tank tops we made quite a scene as we raided the convenience store. We paid in cash so no one would know our names.

We arrived at Amelia Island about 20 minutes later and looked for signs to the Ritz Carlton. Distracted by our chatter, we missed the turn. Realizing we were lost, we decided to at least head toward the water since the hotel was beachfront. We would find it eventually. In the distance we spotted a large hotel with a beautiful blue roof and turned toward it.

"I'd like to stay at a place like that just once before I die," Jennifer remarked. Hoping that we might find the Ritz in the area of that beautiful building, we drove toward it. As we approached, we finally saw signs directing us to the Ritz Carlton. Making one last turn, we suddenly discovered that the large hotel with the blue roof *was actually* The Ritz Carlton!

I stopped the car just short of the entrance.

"I feel completely outclassed," I whispered as I looked at my old shorts and tank top. And Jennifer still had not shaved her legs. Not knowing what else to do, I shifted the car into drive and slowly approached the hotel.

An army of uniformed attendants descended upon the car. "Welcome to the Ritz Carlton. May we get your bags? Please let me valet park your car while you check in. Did you have a pleasant trip?"

Walking inside, Jennifer and I surveyed the tall ceilings, the ornate furnishings, the fresh flowers, and the strict attention to detail. Just then a nicely dressed bellman brought our luggage cart into the lobby. Glancing over, I realized that the oversized bag of cheese puffs had pushed through the top of our brown bag of snacks. The bag rustled loudly as the cart moved.

I wanted to register under an alias!

Jennifer, meanwhile, used the "*I think I'll stand off to the side and pretend I don't know her*" approach. After all, the room was in my name and new one even knew Jennifer Huycke existed.

"Laugh on, Jennifer," I thought to myself. "At least my legs are freshly shaven!"

The bellman led us to our accommodations on the sixth floor. The foyer opened into a suite that was easily larger than my first apartment. The sitting room was decorated beautifully in tones of green with an overstuffed sofa and chairs and a large color television. A separate bedroom was equally posh with two queen beds, desks, and a tall armoire holding another large television. An immense hallway held two large closets complete with thick terry cloth Ritz Carlton robes. There was also a safe for our valuables (maybe the cheese puffs?). A large private balcony overlooked the beach and a perfectly manicured courtyard. Three separate marble bathrooms completed the ensemble.

"Are your accommodations suitable, Mrs. Phillips?" the bellman asked.

"Perfectly," I replied.

When he left the room, Jennifer and I squealed with delight. The place was gorgeous and it was ours for the next three days!

"Where is the phone?" Jennifer shrieked. "I have to call Dick and tell him about this place!"

We looked around the suite and found a variety of phones, six in all. Choosing one next to the sofa, Jennifer remarked, "Wow, look at all the buttons on this phone. I wonder what they all do."

"Just don't call Alaska or do anything to embarrass me," I instructed, remembering that the registration was in my name only.

Lifting the receiver, Jennifer punched in a series of numbers that connected her with the parsonage in Cherokee County. Dick was not home but, in our excitement, we proceeded to leave a very long, very silly message describing our arrival at the Ritz Carlton. With great animation we related everything -- from the uniformed attendants meeting our car to the orange bag of cheese puffs wafting through the lobby on our luggage cart. Jennifer described the room in detail – from the posh furnishings to the magnificent view.

While she talked, I explored the suite and found, to my amazement, that each bathroom was equipped with a telephone. It hung on the wall next to the toilet. So, as Jennifer continued to babble, I picked up the extension from the bathroom in the foyer and said, "Hey, Dick, I am using the phone in the bathroom. Just think, I can go to the bathroom and talk to you at the same time. This phone is in bathroom number one. You don't believe me? Well, I'll prove it."

And I held the receiver at an angle that would pick up the sound of the toilet as I flushed it. Continuing with this theme, I walked into the next bathroom.

"Hello, Dick. I am in bathroom number two. It has a gray marbled floor, a large tub, and a mirror that covers the whole wall. And guess what? There is a phone next to this toilet, too! Just listen."

And I flushed toilet number two.

"Dick, this is me in bathroom number three. We have another marble floor and a shower with a glass door. There are tons of towels and Ritz Carlton toiletries. And, of course, there is a phone. Listen to this!"

And I flushed toilet number three.

Jennifer and I were red-faced with laughter by the time we completed our bizarre message. We were having a great time!

"Now, I've just got to call Mom," and Jennifer again began pushing buttons on the large phone. Before the connection was made, however, she stopped, turned pale, and placed the receiver on the base.

"What?" I demanded. "What's wrong?"

For a few brief seconds she was completely quiet, still pale. Then she spoke in a subdued voice.

"Someone from the hotel office spoke to me when I began dialing," she relayed. "I could hear giggling in the background as they gave me some phone instructions."

"What instructions?" I practically shouted.

Still pale and obviously horrified, Jennifer said, "They told me that, before I made my next call, I should depress the conference call button. And they called me *Mrs. Phillips.*"

This meant only one thing – the staff in the hotel office had heard our entire ridiculous, absurd, laughable conversation. I turned pale myself. Jennifer was obviously telling the truth. I knew her – she would never have used the word "depress." She would have used "push or press" instead. She's a kindergarten teacher, after all!

For me, the most awful part of this nightmare was that the operator had called her *Mrs. Phillips.* The Ritz Carlton did not know Jennifer at all; they only knew the room was registered to *Mrs. Phillips.* They even knew my home address and my credit card number.

"I'm never leaving this room," I said, completely humiliated.

Jennifer confessed, "I think I want to go home."

Silence filled the room -- at least for a few minutes before Jennifer began a soft giggle that quickly matured into a loud belly laugh. It took me a few minutes longer to see the humor in the situation because, I was, after all, *Mrs. Phillips*, the registered guest.

We laughed until our sides hurt. We laughed until we rolled off the sofa and onto the dark green carpet. We laughed until tears rolled down our faces. We laughed until we each had to use one of the three bathrooms in the suite.

"These people will think we are just two naïve preacher's wives from the country," Jennifer pouted.

"We are," I said, and the laughter began all over again.

Happily, we did not go home, nor did we hide in our room for the rest of our trip. We took full advantage of the hotel's amenities – the swimming pools, the hot tubs, the beautiful beach and gardens. We enjoyed high tea in a cozy setting overlooking the ocean. We even found the courage to use the telephone again. Our three days passed so quickly that leaving was difficult and we promised ourselves we would return one day.

Luckily, I have returned many times since that first trip to the Ritz Carlton. In fact, it is my favorite get-away! At no time, though, has the hotel refused my reservation because of the behavior Jennifer and I exhibited on our first visit. On the contrary, each trip to the Ritz Carlton is wonderful and I return home rested in body and spirit.

No trip quite compares to the first, of course. After months of grief and depression, I experienced real laughter again – not a wimpy little chuckle, but a body-aching, bladder-clenching, tear-producing belly laugh.

God, it felt wonderful!

There is a time for everything,
and a season for every activity under heaven:
a time to be born and a time to die,
a time to plant and a time to uproot,
a time to tear down and a time to build,
a time to weep and a time to LAUGH,
a time to mourn and a time to dance.

Ecclesiastes 3:1-4
(NIV)

THE ALMOND JOY INCIDENT

Author's Note:

This true story took place in 1989 while Jerry served as Pastor of Orange United Methodist Church in Lathemtown, Georgia. All people and events are completely real and members of the congregation still laughingly remind me of this incident whenever I am able to visit them.

My dear friend, Ray Lathem, asked me many times, "Have you written our story yet?" I finally did write our story and took a copy of it to him. He laughed heartily and showed it proudly to his family and neighbors. This article was originally published in the November/December 1997 issue of Today's Christian Woman Magazine. Oddly enough, I received the acceptance letter from Today's Christian Woman on the very day Ray passed away following a long-term illness. I miss my friend, Ray, but I know he now has a perfect body and that he and Jerry are continuing the deep friendship they began in this lifetime.

I am happy to report that "The Almond Joy Incident" won First Place in the 1997 Humor Article Category from the Evangelical Press Association Higher Goals in Christian Journalism Award. My sincere appreciation is extended to Today's Christian Woman for their publication of the story in 1997. The story is dedicated to all my fellow dieters!

THE ALMOND JOY INCIDENT

It all started with a simple glass of water. It was Day fourteen of my Weight Watchers Diet, and I was doing great! I'd lost seven pounds by carefully keeping track of my food exchanges. For two weeks I'd successfully avoided hamburgers and cheesecake. I was following the regime religiously in all areas but one – I simply couldn't drink eight glasses of water a day. Impossible! I could never get further than glass number six. I spent the rest of the day trotting to the nearest bathroom.

Nevertheless, on this particular Saturday, I was determined that nothing would deter me from consuming the prescribed eight glasses. Nothing! So I panicked at 11:36 p.m. when I realized I'd only had seven glasses of water. Only twenty-four meager minutes until midnight. Could I do it?

Despite the late hour and the danger of bladder-related sleep deprivation, I braced myself for one more glass of water. In the kitchen I grabbed a glass and sliced a fresh, juicy lemon. The nightmare began when I opened the freezer for a few cubes of ice. It was lying there, innocently tucked behind a few stray cartons of frozen yogurt and two packs of Weight Watchers frozen lasagna. How it got there is still a mystery. I only know that my eyes grew wide and my heart beat wildly.

An Almond Joy! Two simple bits of coconut, each bathed in milk chocolate and crowned with a large crunchy almond, swaddled in a beautiful blue wrapper. An Almond Joy!

Rationalization was easy. I'd been on my diet for two weeks and had lost seven pounds. Surely one simple candy bar wouldn't harm me. I probably needed the sugar in my system after not having had any for, lo, those fourteen days. And it was an awfully hot night so the candy bar would be especially cool and refreshing. Besides, it wasn't as if I'd been looking for an Almond Joy. On the contrary, the Almond Joy had found me.

Best of all, my husband, Jerry, was sleeping soundly. He would never know. No one would ever know. It was all so perfect. Surely it was God's will that I eat this Almond Joy!

Grabbing the candy bar and my Number Eight glass of water, I raced for the sofa. I crossed my legs underneath me, aimed the TV remote, and found a *MASH* rerun. Perfect! Quite deliberately I unwrapped my new-found treasure from its bright blue cover and held it aloft. Life was suddenly very exciting.

The candy bar was frozen but not too firm against my teeth. It was cool and sweet. And it was all mine. No one would ever know that I'd surrendered my diet for this piece of heaven that had so unexpectedly entered my life.

I ate it all. Every bit of chocolate, every dab of coconut, every crumb of almond. And because I had something to eat, it was so much easier to drink my Number Eight glass of water.

Turning off the TV, I placed my empty glass in the sink and popped the bright blue wrapper in the trashcan. Risking a mouthful of cavities, I didn't even stop to brush my teeth. I fell asleep with the taste of Almond Joy still dancing in my mouth.

My husband, Pastor of Orange United Methodist Church, awoke early the next morning to put the finishing touches on his sermon. While I slept soundly, he puttered in the kitchen, toasting some bread and pouring himself a tall glass of orange juice. Emptying the carton, he opened the pantry door and reached for the garbage can. The bag was full. As he bent to remove it, Jerry discovered the remains of a bright blue Almond Joy wrapper perched atop the other miscellaneous garbage.

What is this? He thought to himself. He didn't remember eating a candy bar. And knowing I was religiously following the Weight Watchers Diet, he was puzzled by the object that had somehow found its way into our garbage can. Clutching the wrapper to his chest, he walked quietly back to the bedroom where I slept, unaware of the trouble at hand.

"Cathy," he nudged me gently. Opening one eye slowly, I looked into his loving face. He smiled at me. I smiled back. Was he feeling romantic at this hour? And on a Sunday morning? Then, almost immediately, I caught sight of a familiar bright blue piece of paper in his hand. Could it be? Jerry dangled the wrapper above me, a clever smirk on his face.

"Do you want to tell me about this?" he asked. The smirk grew larger.

It wasn't that my husband noticed every pound I gained or lost. He loved me regardless of my weight or the number of Almond Joys I might consume. I knew that without question.

It was the smirk.

That arrogant little grin told me that my late-night escapade was no longer my little secret. I'd been found out.

So, why not just admit I'd found an Almond Joy and, in a moment of weakness, had eaten it? I knew I should have told the truth, but in the heat of the moment I panicked. I can only blame my actions on the "sinful" chocolate in my stomach and the smirk on my husband's face.

"The candy bar belonged to Ray Lathem," I blurted.

Ray Lathem, a good friend of ours and member of our church, lived across the street from our parsonage. Recently Ray had been placed on a strict eating program by his doctor, so he and I often shared our dieting successes and failures. I knew, therefore, that Ray would understand my Almond Joy experience. I would tell him about it after church and we would have a good laugh together.

"Last night, Ray Lathem knocked on our door," the lie began. "He'd been craving a candy bar all day but knew his family would never let him have one. Finally, he couldn't stand it! In a moment of weakness, he ate an Almond Joy he'd hidden in his truck. But he didn't know what to do with the wrapper. If his wife found it, she'd know he'd abandoned his diet. So Ray sneaked out of the his house and knocked on our door. He had one simple request: Could he place the wrapper in our garbage can? What could I do? Of course I would let my friend and fellow dieter place the wrapper in our garbage can," I concluded with great emotion.

"That's your story?" Jerry's smirk filled the room.

"And I'm sticking to it," I replied, rather proud of the creativity I'd exhibited at such an early hour. I pulled the blanket over my head while Jerry, chuckling loudly, returned to his sermon and orange juice.

I put the story out of my mind until 11:35 a.m. when Jerry, beginning his sermon, reached inside his pocket and held the familiar wrapper before the entire congregation.

"Ray Lathem, does this belong to you?" the voice from the pulpit inquired.

Ray and his wife, Leila, were in their usual pew. Confused, Ray looked innocently at Leila, begging to be believed.

Knowing I had a sense of humor, my husband relayed the story to the entire congregation. He then thanked me for providing the perfect illustration for his sermon entitled, appropriately enough, "The Devil Made Me Do It." The congregation laughed and laughed. And they kept laughing. In fact, Ray laughed the loudest, delighted that I'd included him in my elaborate tale.

Afterwards, many people came up to me saying that I was a good sport for being able to laugh at myself. And, before the day was done, more than two dozen Almond Joys had been brought to our home by sympathetic friends who themselves had fallen off the diet wagon at least once. With his wife's permission, I shared the goods with Ray Lathem.

During his sermon, Jerry shared the passage in Numbers 32 in which Moses told the Israelites that their sins would find them out. Jerry said our sins would always find us out sooner or later, too.

Mine sure did. I just pray I can learn to limit my sins to Almond Joys.

Behold, you have sinned against the Lord,
and be sure your sin will find you out.

Numbers 32:23
(New American Standard)

CONSIDER THE BIRDS OF THE AIR

January 12, 1992

What was it that woke me from a sound sleep?

Opening one eye I glanced at the clock. 5:52 a.m. – almost a full hour before the alarm would sound to begin a very busy Sunday. Almost immediately my mind began to enumerate the things I had to do . . .

- ✓ Get up and get dressed
- ✓ Gas up the car
- ✓ Stop by St. Joseph's Hospital for a morning visit with Jerry
- ✓ Get to church on time
- ✓ Present the children's sermon – I had no idea what I was going to do
- ✓ Direct the adult choir for the 11:00 a.m. service
- ✓ Meet Dick and Jennifer for lunch
- ✓ Stop by Wal-Mart for shampoo and laundry detergent
- ✓ Rush back to the hospital for a few more hours with Jerry

- ✓ Complete a typing job I had taken on to earn a few extra dollars
- ✓ Pay some bills
- ✓ Wash several loads of laundry
- ✓ Gather up leaves in the yard
- ✓ Make a few phone calls
- ✓ Try to get to bed before Monday morning!

This would be a very long day and I wanted those extra precious minutes of sleep! Turning over, I punched my pillow and slid deeper under the covers. Ah . . . finally, the perfect comfort zone. Surely I would fall asleep quickly and take full advantage of those remaining moments before the alarm growled at me.

Instead, my mind wandered. I was in our own bed in our home in Atlanta. We had purchased our home years ago, before Jerry had been recently assigned to serve Orange United Methodist Church near Canton, Georgia. Though the church provided us with a beautiful parsonage, I usually stayed in our Atlanta home when Jerry was hospitalized. It was only seven miles from St. Joseph's Hospital. The church, however, was forty-five minutes away. Nevertheless, I tried to be at church each Sunday to express my gratitude to this congregation that had loved us so unselfishly.

As my thoughts rambled, the noise that had obviously awakened me grew louder. What was it? A growl? A roar? A hum? I didn't care. I simply wanted to sleep.

The noise increased and I realized my attempt at sleep was futile. Besides, my curiosity had been aroused. Shivering in the January air, I grabbed my robe and went in search of the mysterious noise. Climbing the stairs I prayed that some major appliance had not decided to die, thus presenting me with a large repair bill. Or maybe the old furnace had decided to quit today, one of the coldest days of the year. I paused at the top of the stairs before walking into the living room. Then, I jumped as a sudden movement outside the window startled me. Astonished, I stared at our front lawn.

Birds! Hundreds of them! They were everywhere, covering practically every square inch of our half-acre lot. Where had they come from? Where were they going? And why had they stopped in our yard? Had they schemed to rob me of a few precious minutes of sleep.

I was intrigued and despite the cold temperatures, I opened the front door. Pulling my robe close, I sat behind the storm door and watched this surprising show of nature. I quickly realized why the birds had paused at our address. Dead leaves – one of the great frustrations of my life. Jerry and I loved the beautiful hardwoods that covered our wooded lot in Atlanta. Or, more correctly, we loved them three out of the four seasons. In autumn, these beautiful trees dropped thousands of dead leaves that had to be raked, bagged, and dropped at the curb in a mound of black bags. It was backbreaking work that had mostly gone unattended this particular year.

In October, just as the leaves began to fall, Jerry had entered St. Joseph's Hospital with a severe rejection of his heart. He had undergone a heart transplant in May 1990 and had encountered very few problems. However, this rejection was stubborn and he spent several weeks in Intensive Care as doctors struggled to halt the rejection. My days were spent balancing work, church, and hospital duty, which left little time for raking leaves. Yes, I worried that the neighbors would report me to the "yard police" but, under the circumstances, dead leaves were just not a priority for me.

But they were most certainly a priority for these birds. Fascinated, I watched as they pecked and scratched the ground. Twigs and leaves were tossed into the air as the birds feasted on the various worms and bugs hiding underneath. There was a virtual "bird buffet" being served right in our own backyard!

Look at the birds of the air, that they do not sow, neither do they reap, nor gather into barns, and yet your heavenly Father feeds them. Are you not worth much more than they? (Matthew 6:26, New American Standard).

That verse which had brought me great comfort so often, jumped into my mind. God was, indeed, feeding the birds, just as He had promised. And, even more miraculously, He was using the dead leaves that had been such a headache for me for many weeks. The leaves sheltered the worms and insects that provided nourishment for these birds on their journey. Proof of God's faithfulness was taking place right before my eyes. Perhaps that is why I sat and watched for a long time; I felt that God was showing me something very extraordinary that was far more than simple coincidence.

As the birds filled their stomachs and took their leave, I quickly showered and dressed for the day. Running to my car, I scooped up a handful of dead leaves and twigs and placed them into a clear, plastic bag. I had my children's sermon for the day. Using Matthew 6:26, I would tell them of how, in that early morning hour, I watched God care for the birds.

******

Rushing into Jerry's hospital room, I was pleased to find him standing at the sink shaving and washing his face. For so long he had been too weak to get out of bed. But he was growing stronger each day. He remained in the hospital because doctors, while taking a routine chest x-ray two days earlier, had found a small spot on his lung. It was winter and because his immune system had been suppressed to halt the rejection of his heart, the doctors believed the spot to be a simple touch of pneumonia. Jerry would undergo a series of tests the next day and, hopefully, be home by the middle of the week. We were both looking forward to his return home. Finally, we would resume a normal life.

While Jerry shaved, I related the story of the birds. We both recognized that God had miraculously used our unkept lawn to accomplish the promise found in Matthew 6:26. And because we were more important than birds, we knew that God would care for us, too.

Jerry and I both felt God especially close to us that morning. A yard filled with birds and a few quiet moments together helped us put the stress of recent weeks in perspective. Whether in the hospital or out, God would take care of Jerry. And His love for me was just as steadfast. "Do not be anxious," the Scripture said.

I had been very anxious while Jerry was in the ill. *Yes, God,* I thought, *I will try to be less anxious and more trusting of your care for us.*

* * * * * * *

Orange United Methodist Church, Lathemtown, Georgia. Jerry had been serving this church when he received word that he needed a new heart. He was suffering from cardiomyopathy, a disease of the heart muscle. A transplant was his only hope for life.

The congregation of this wonderful church proved to be a family to us. They prayed with us. They visited us. They called daily to keep Jerry's spirits up. They called daily to keep my spirits up. They brought food, money, and gifts of encouragement. And, during the early morning hours of Jerry's transplant, many filled the waiting room, leaving only after his surgery was over and he was stable. I am still awed and amazed at the love they provided during those frightening days. It is something that can never be fully repaid.

Naturally, they were greatly concerned when Jerry returned to the hospital with rejection of his heart. And on this Sunday morning, as always, they wanted an update on "Brother Jerry" during the morning service.

"He's doing much better," I told them. "He has what probably is a slight case of pneumonia but should be home by the middle of the week." They rejoiced with me at the good news. And they listened intently as I told the children of the goodness of God in feeding the birds that cold January morning.

I left the church just after 12:00 and met my friends, Dick and Jennifer, for lunch. Leaving the restaurant, I rushed to Wal-Mart and then back to the hospital to spent the rest of the afternoon with Jerry.

My husband and I spent the afternoon talking and snuggling in his hospital bed. We read the Sunday paper and even looked through the pet section. I wanted a new puppy and we were trying to pick out the best breed for us. It was a wonderful afternoon but, sensing my fatigue, Jerry sent me home around 5:00 p.m. I was tired and I had that typing job to finish, but I was reluctant to leave. I had almost lost him. Each moment was precious. He was insistent, though. Walking toward my car, I felt an overwhelming urge to return to his room for one more "I love you."

"I love you, too, sweet," He smiled. "I'll see you in the morning."

* * * * * * *

Silver In The Slop

The call came at 7:45 p.m.

"Come to the hospital immediately," I was instructed. Jerry had suffered a cardiac arrest.

Though the drive was only seven miles, it seemed to take forever. A chaplain met me at the front door and escorted me to the nurse's station just outside Jerry's room. The activity was intense – doctors and nurses ran in and out of the room I had left only hours before. As they opened the door, I could see Jerry lying on the floor. A doctor was administering CPR. The scene was surreal. I was completely numb. A nurse finally placed her arm around me and escorted me to a private waiting room. Within minutes a doctor appeared who spoke the words that would change my life forever: "We couldn't bring him back."

A blood clot had lodged in Jerry's pulmonary artery. His death was instantaneous. Jerry never had pneumonia. The spots in his lungs were small blood clots that had originated in his legs. They had begun to break up and move throughout his body. Most were small but the one that traveled to the pulmonary artery that night was large enough to end his life.

I was completely calm because I was completely numb. My mind was unable to process the information it had just received. A terrible mistake had been made. I was sure of it. Jerry was not dead – it was another patient instead.

In a few moments, people began to arrive. Family and friends. Other ministers. Members of our church.

Finally, I was taken into Jerry's room. I spent time alone with him and, from time to time, others came in to be with me. It was well after midnight before Toni and Bill Jernigan took me home. Jennifer came over, as well, and knowing that I would probably not sleep, she climbed into bed with me and we began to talk.

Had it only that morning that a strange noise had awakened me and I discovered the mass of birds in our yard? It seemed an eternity ago. In the darkness, I shared the story with Jennifer and God's promise from Matthew again entered my mind. God takes care of the birds. I had seen it for myself that very morning. Likewise, God would surely take care of me.

And in the dark of the terrifying night, I remembered another time Jesus spoke of the birds of the air:

Are not two sparrows sold for a cent? And yet not one of them will fall to the ground apart from your Father. But the very hairs of your head are all numbered. Therefore do not fear; you are of more value than many sparrows." (Matthew 10:29-30, New American Standard).

One of God's own had fallen. Though Jerry was no longer with me, I knew he was fine; I knew that without question.

But was I okay? Certainly was not at that moment. And though there would be many long, difficult, lonely days ahead, I would be okay again.

You see, God does care for the bird that has fallen. But His love is just as great for the ones still flying!

But someone will say, "How are the dead raised? And with what kind of body do they come? You fool! That which you sow does not come to life unless it dies;"

I Corinthians 15: 35-36
(New American Standard)

ABOUT THE AUTHOR

Cathy Lee Phillips is a native of Newnan, Georgia, a rapidly growing city just south of Atlanta. Newnan is also home of the late humorist Lewis Grizzard, and country music singers Alan Jackson and Doug Stone.

Following her graduation from Newnan High School in 1974, Cathy attended LaGrange College where she earned a double major in Religion and Spanish. She graduated Summa cum Laude in 1978. Cathy was offered a Presidential Merit Award to attend Scarritt College in Nashville, Tennessee, where she earned a Master's Degree in Christian Education from this United Methodist College. While a student at Scarritt, Cathy served as President of the Student Government Association and was elected as a Graduate Assistant with the Department of Christian Education. She graduated with honors in 1980.

Returning to Georgia, Cathy served Atlanta's Grace United Methodist Church as Director of Children and Family Ministries (1980-1984), Kingswood United Methodist Church as Director of Christian Education (1984-1985), and St. James United Methodist Church as Director of Youth and Activities Ministry (1985-1990). In 1990, she accepted a position in the business world and is currently General Manager of American

Photographic Services, Inc., in the Lake Hartwell area of South Carolina.

In 1986, Cathy married Dr. Jerry E. Phillips, an ordained Minister in the United Methodist Church (North Georgia Conference). They were married until Jerry's death in 1992. His death was a result of complications related to a heart transplant he received in May 1990 at St. Joseph's Hospital in Atlanta. Since her husband's transplant, Cathy has been an advocate and frequent speaker regarding the need for organ donation.

A published writer, Cathy's articles have appeared in Angels on Earth (A Guideposts Publication), Today's Christian Woman, Photo Lab Management, The Wesleyan Christian Advocate, and the Newnan Times Herald. At the request of the Editors at Guideposts, Cathy recently taped a 30-minute program for North Georgia Television to discuss her "grief journey" following her husband's death.

Though no longer serving the church in a professional capacity, Cathy remains committed to the ministry of the United Methodist Church. She has volunteered as a Sunday School Teacher, Pianist, Choir Director, and Retreat Leader. Putting to use several years of vocal instruction, she is a frequent soloist in local churches. In addition, Cathy is a popular retreat leader and speaker for church, business, educational, and civic groups regarding her life, her work, and the lessons she has learned along the way.

Cathy recently moved just north of Atlanta to the outskirts of Canton, Georgia. In her "spare time" Cathy enjoys writing, singing, spending time with friends, playing basketball, or simply sitting on the patio with her new Golden Retriever (mostly), Shadow, and watching the sun go down!

Cathy Lee Phillips is available as a retreat leader, program leader, speaker, or soloist for your church, business, educational, or civic group. She will be happy to work with you in preparing programs geared to the specific needs of your group. Feel free to contact her!

Cathy Lee Phillips
Patchwork Press, Ltd.
P. O. Box 4684
Canton, Georgia 30115
www.patchworkpress.com

Order Books Today!

Patchwork Press, Ltd.
P. O. Box 4684
Canton, Georgia 30115
770-720-7988 - www.patchworkpress.com

Prices Effective August 1, 2003 (Prices Include Tax)

Silver in the Slop: ____ copies @ $12 each = _______

Gutsy Little Flowers: ____ copies @ $13 each = ______

Silver Reflections Daily Journal: _____ copies @ $13 each = ______

Aging, Ailments, and Attitudes: _____ copies @ $17 each = ______

Shipping and Handling: __________
($ 1.00 per book ordered)

Total Amount of Order: __________

....

Make checks payable to Patchwork Press, Ltd.,
or pay by Visa, MasterCard, or Discover.

Credit Card Number:______________________________________
Name of Cardholder:______________________________________
Expiration Date:___________ Signature:____________________

....

Please Ship Books to:

Name:____
Address:____
City:________________State:___________Zip: _________
Phone:______________E-Mail: ______________________